The title of this book ~~~~~~~~~~~~~~~~~ of the blood that runs through Mark Hallock's and Scott Iken's veins. Their relentless commitment to lift-up, build-up, and fire-up those around them is a gospel-inspired infection and not, as many believe, a personality type. Mark and Scott take us inside the Scriptures and behind the curtain of their experience to expose the gospel's power to grow that same contagious spirit in each of us. Prepare to become an infectious encourager as you read this book.

Jim Misloski, *Developing Leader Director of the Missouri Baptist Convention*

Mark and Scott do an excellent job of fleshing out what it means to be sincere, relentless, encouragers as they look at what motivates our hearts to speak the words we choose. Each chapter beautifully displays how true biblical encouragement is not just flattery, but rather, it flows from a heart that has been transformed by the grace of Christ. This is a helpful read for teens through adults and practically addresses how we can be disciplined in making the words of our mouths pleasing to God, reflecting hearts that have been truly changed by the gospel, for the purpose of uplifting and encouraging others for the glory of God.

Kirsten Black, *Women's Ministry Director, Acts 29 U.S. West*

This is a great little book about a great big need and I cannot imagine two better men to write it than Mark Hallock and Scott Iken. If there was such a thing as an encouragement coach, these guys would be the best in the business and now we can all benefit from their study, experience, and hearts. Whether you are a leader, spouse, teacher, friend, neighbor or just someone who knows people, read this book and use it to bless others.

Adam Fix, *Pastor, Our Saviour Church, Wheeling, Illinois*

The Relentless Encourager is a balm for our day. In this age of toxic hot-takes, Hallock and Iken bring us back to the goodness of encouraging words. The message of the book carries the reader from conviction to inspiration—from reminders of what's true and right, to practical tools and ideas for becoming an encourager. This is not a how-to book, but rather an exploration of the Word of God, a reminder of the necessary equipping of the Spirit of God, and an exhortation to the people of God to live on mission through our words. Oh, that we may see an awakening of kindness and encouragement in the church and radiating from it! This book will help us get there

Jen Oshman, *Author of* Enough About Me: Find Lasting Joy in the Age of Self

We were made in the image of God, with the purpose of glorifying God in all that we do and *say*. Often times, however, the small rudder in our mouth has shifted the direction of the entire vessel that embodies the Spirit of God. Mark and Scott have written an important work with pointed clarity and concise application that encourages and convicts simultaneously. May each of us train our tongues to truly reveal our hearts that are yielded to God and maturing in His likeness.

Ray Garcia, *Pastor, Roxborough Church; Executive Director, Philadelphia Project, Philadelphia, PA*

In this short but substantial book, Mark and Scott take the often oversimplified topic of encouragement to a deeper level. Many people struggle to get past behavior modification, but this book does a fantastic job of looking *inward* with provoking, heart-level questions and *outward* with strategic tools to help anyone grow in encouragement. A necessary read!

Rachel Haley, *Licensed Professional Counselor*

Barnabas, the Son of Encouragement, it seems has two brothers in authors Mark Hallock and Scott Iken! This wonderfully practical, Gospel-centered, Word-saturated book puts courage into its readers to be relentless encouragers of others. Highly recommended!

Chris Durkin, *Pastor, Colts Neck Community Church, Colts Neck, New Jersey*

THE RELENTLESS
ENCOURAGER

the Relentless encourager

MARK HALLOCK
& SCOTT IKEN

ACOMA PRESS

Scott – To my wife and kids. You all are such a gift from God. Thanks for faithfully encouraging me.

Mark - To my mom and dad, who have been the two most encouraging people in my life. Thanks for always building me up with your words.

CONTENTS

ACKNOWLEDGMENTS

Scott - I would like to first and foremost thank the Lord. I am ever encouraged that You first loved me. I am so grateful for my amazing wife, Pam and my sweet kids, Addi, Seth, Reis, and Sadie. Thanks to my kind parents, Cliff and Kathy. I am thankful for my terrific friend, Mark. Special thanks to all the Calvary Family of Church Pastors.

Mark – I want to thank my wife, Jenna, and my kids, Zoe and Eli. You three bring so much joy and encouragement to my life. I also want to thank the church staff at Calvary Church Englewood. You all are some of the greatest encouragers I have ever met. I praise God every day for the blessing of getting to serve with each of you. Finally, I want to thank the Lord, the Great Encourager, who lifts us up in the deepest valleys of our lives. I'm more than grateful.

INTRODUCTION

There's nothing more powerful—as leaders, as parents, as Christians—than becoming relentless encouragers of people. Those who lovingly and joyfully encourage for the glory of God and the building up of others. But what exactly is encouragement? It's not a topic we read or talk about very often.

And that is a problem.

In fact, the sad reality is, while discouragement abounds in our world and in our lives, encouragement is quite rare. Why don't we encourage others much? What's holding us back? Can we grow as encouragers? How can we begin to practice life-giving encouragement in the way God's Word calls us to? We hope that through considering the answers to questions like these, by the end of this book you'll be able to say, *"God has made me to be an encourager of others…and it's my joy to do so!"*

Friends, the truth is this: If you are a Christian, the Lord has shown you amazing grace upon grace. Through the saving work of Jesus Christ on our behalf, we have been forgiven, set free, justified, adopted as sons and daughters of God! What grace! So, how should we respond to such grace, specifically with the words we speak? The Lord tells us through the Apostle Paul:

> "For God did not appoint us to wrath, but to obtain salvation through our Lord Jesus Christ, who died for us, so that whether we are awake or asleep, we may live together with Him. Therefore encourage one another and build each other up..." - 1 Thessalonians 5:9-11.

Encourage one another and build each other up! This should be the overflow of our lives and our lips because of the Lord's amazing grace toward us. In fact, because of the kindness and encouragement God has shown us through Jesus, the question we should now be asking as Christians is this: *"How can I **not** be an encourager of others? How can I **not** use my words to build others up?"* Our prayer for you and for us is that as we grow together in our understanding and practice of speaking words of genuine encouragement, the Lord will do incredible things in us and through us for His glory, that others' lives will be changed through His mighty power!

As we begin the short journey through this book together, let's pray and ask our great God to do a work in us that only He can do:

Father, we come before you humbly and with great joy and expectation. Teach us as we study Your Word and submit to Your Holy Spirit. And we pray, God, that You would do the work in us that You desire to do. Here's what we know: all of us fall short in so many ways. This includes the ways we often fall short in honoring You and edifying others with our words. We pray that by Your grace, You would help us to grow in the area of encouragement. You would convict us in ways that we need to be convicted. You would encourage us in the ways we need to be encouraged. Lord, continue to sanctify us and make us a people that brings glory to Your name and life to others through the words we speak. Mold us into the people You desire us to be, those who relentlessly encourage others as You so endlessly encourage us. We pray this in Jesus' name. Amen.

PART 1:

THE NEED
FOR RELENTLESS
ENCOURAGERS

why our words MATTER

"Sticks and stones may break my bones, but words will never hurt me."

Words will never hurt me. Really? Is this true? What do you think about this statement?

I (Mark) remember learning this little rhyme all the way back in preschool. Perhaps you did too. My guess is that like me, you have found this little rhyme to be anything but true. My hunch is that also like me, you have been hurt by others' words on multiple occasions throughout your life. In fact, I'm quite sure that even as you read this you can remember a time in your life in which somebody said something negative, something hurtful to you, and it stuck to your heart and mind like glue. Perhaps you still regularly think about those painful words to this very day, years or even decades later. Mean and hurtful things that have shaped who you are. Or at least who you think you are.

Perhaps the deepest wounds are from those things people we loved and looked up to, *didn't* say. The words they didn't encourage us with. The words they didn't counsel us with. The words they didn't speak to spur us on with.

At the same time, as much as we have all been affected negatively by discouraging, demeaning words from others, we have also been helped by encouraging words from those who sought to build us up, those who saw good things in us that no one had ever brought to light before. These are the kinds of words that bring life. They bring hope. They help us to see who we really are in Christ. To see that God loves us, is with us, and is working in our lives for His glory and our joy in Him. This is the power of encouragement.

SETTING A BIBLICAL FRAMEWORK
FOR RELENTLESS ENCOURAGEMENT

The reality is this. We all know that little "sticks and stones" rhyme simply isn't true. It is a lie. Words will hurt you. And our words will hurt others. But our words also have the power to heal others too. In fact, our words have the power to bring deep comfort and joy to those around us. More than that, as Christians, we were redeemed by Jesus to be people who bring life, hope, and healing to people through our words. Not the opposite. I can tell you this, every person we meet and interact with today needs words of encouragement. Every single one. And guess what? God made us to be the relentless deliverers of these words of life. Speaking words of encouragement ought not be viewed as a duty for us, but rather an absolute delight!

God gave us words for a reason. Namely, that we might speak life-giving, joy-producing, God-glorifying words that build people up and point others to Him. As we get started, let's consider three foundational, biblical convictions regarding the words that we speak. These three convictions will help set a biblical and theological framework for where we're going through the remainder of this book.

Conviction #1: God gave us words that we might glorify Him through them.

"So, whether you eat or drink, or whatever you do, do all to the glory of God."
- 1 Corinthians 10:31

The Apostle Paul lays out for us here a principle and truth that applies to every part of our lives. God is to be glorified in and through us! We see this theme of the glory of God from Genesis to Revelation, for God alone is worthy to be glorified in all things. Of course, this includes our words and how we speak to others. Because of this, as those who have been saved and redeemed through the grace of God, we have been remade in Christ to be people who speak words that encourage people, that love people, that build up others—ultimately, that God might be glorified.

The Lord is worthy to be glorified in our words of praise to Him and our words of affirmation to others. So from the very beginning, we must understand that central in this whole discussion of words, and specifically words of encouragement, is the glory of God. We need to take encouragement seriously; the glory of God is at stake in this.

Conviction #2: Our words have great power to bring harm or healing to others.

Words are far more powerful than any of us realize. They can be life giving and life changing; or they can be life damaging and life destroying. Listen to these verses and the descriptions used from the book of Proverbs on the power of our words:

> Anxiety in a man's heart leads him down, but a good word makes him glad. - Proverbs 12:25

> For gracious words are like a honeycomb, sweetness to the soul and health to the body. - Proverbs 16:24

> The tongue that brings healing is a tree of life, but a deceitful tongue crushes the spirit. - Proverbs 15:4

> "Death and life are in the power of the tongue." - Proverbs 18:21a

Death and life are two strong words. This proverb tells us that our words can kill. Think about that for a second. That is serious. Our words have within them the power to bring absolute death and darkness to others. But our words also have the power to bring life and light. The tongue is powerful. How will we use it?

Conviction #3: Our words reveal what is going on in our hearts.

The overarching theme of the book of James is this: if you're a Christian, if you have truly been saved by the life-transforming grace of God, it should flesh itself out in how you live. True saving faith always results in a life that seeks to love God and love others for the glory of God. In other words, if you and I just talk the talk and don't walk the walk when it comes to our faith in Christ, something is really wrong. Something is not right. You see, for those of us who have been born again in Christ, we have been made new. As Paul puts it in 2 Corinthians 5:17, "Therefore, if anyone is in Christ, he is a new creation. The old has passed away; behold, the new has come." The Lord, by His grace and power, has made us new and is now sanctifying us and growing us day by day that we might be conformed to the image of Christ. This work of transformation affects every area of our lives. Every area. This includes a growing desire to speak words of life to other people and words of praise to our Father in heaven. James is right when he says:

> For we all stumble in many ways. And if anyone does not stumble in what he says, he is a perfect man, able also to bridle his whole body. If we put bits into the mouths of horses so that they obey us, we guide their whole bodies as well. Look at the ships also: though they are so large and are driven by strong winds, they are guided by a very small rudder wherever the will of the pilot directs. So also the tongue is a small member, yet it boasts of great things. How great a forest is set ablaze by such a small fire! And the tongue is a fire, a world of unrighteousness. The tongue is set among our members, staining the whole body, setting on fire the entire course of life, and set on fire by hell. For every kind of beast and bird, of reptile and sea creature, can be tamed and has been tamed by mankind, but no human being can tame the tongue. It is a restless evil, full of deadly poison. With it we bless our Lord and Father, and with it we curse people who are made in the likeness of God. From the same mouth come blessing and cursing. My brothers, these things ought not to be so. Does a spring pour forth from the same opening both fresh and salt water? Can a fig tree, my brothers, bear olives, or a grapevine produce figs? Neither can a salt pond yield fresh water. - James 3:2-12

What hits you when you read these verses? Does something stand out to you in what James is communicating here? James clearly wants us to understand that the tongue is powerful and can be used for great good or great harm. But notice how ultimately our words are simply the fruit of what is happening internally. In other words, what we say flows from what is happening in our hearts. James forces us in this passage to ask questions like, "What kind of water is the spring of our heart producing? Is it fresh or is it salty?" And, "What kinds of food is being produced from the tree of our heart? Olives or figs?" This matter of the heart is what Jesus is getting at in Luke 6:45 when he says,

"The good person out of the good treasure of his heart produces good, and the evil person out of his evil treasure produces evil, for out of the abundance of the heart his mouth speaks." - Luke 6:45

Jesus has a lot to say about words. He also has a lot to say about our hearts. Here in Luke 6, he makes it very clear that our words really aren't a mouth issue; they are a heart issue. It isn't really a tongue issue; it's a motives issue. A self-control issue. A love issue.

If we don't understand that the words we speak are really just the overflow of what is happening in our hearts, then all we're doing when we talk about changing how we speak is attempting to modify behavior.

And this never works. Not in a lasting, God-honoring way.

There are many people who falsely believe that if we just discipline ourselves enough, read a self-help book or two on the topic, and work really hard to say nice things to others, then somehow we can transform the way we speak once and for all. But this won't happen. It can't happen apart from a heart that is changed by the power of the Holy Spirit. The only way that we're going to become individuals who speak words of true life and grace is when we allow the Lord to take over our hearts. To transform our hearts. To change our desires, our affections, our passions, our very character, all by His grace alone. Only the Lord can do this in us, and He longs to do so!

SOME WISDOM FROM A 19TH CENTURY PREACHER

In light of the three convictions we have considered regarding our words, let us close with some wisdom from the great British Baptist preacher, Charles Spurgeon. Spurgeon spoke and wrote a great deal on the importance of God-honoring words. In fact, some of the wisest, most helpful teaching on this important topic has come from either the pen or pulpit of this mighty man of God. On a Sunday morning in 1884, Spurgeon addressed the vital connection between our words and our hearts. His words are as timely in our day as they were in his. Spurgeon declared to his congregation,

> The grace of God very speedily sweetens a man's tongue, and if his religion does not operate upon his speech surely it is not the religion of the pure and holy God…

He goes on,

> If the tongue be set on fire of hell the heart is not on fire with grace from heaven. The doctor says, "Put out your tongue," and he judges the symptoms of health or

disease thereby; assuredly, there is no better test of the inward character than the condition of the tongue. [1]

Spurgeon's teaching on the tongue here sounds alot like the teaching of Jesus. As we have seen in this chapter, and what we must remember throughout this book, is that our words are very powerful. Our words are meant to bring glory to God. And ultimately, this whole matter of our words is really a matter of our hearts. Put another way, the condition of our tongue simply reflects the condition of our character. The two are vitally connected.

As we begin to look more closely at the actual words God desires for us to speak, let us stay close to this teaching concerning our hearts. May we remember that our primary focus when it comes to our words must always be the spiritual condition of our hearts. For it is indeed out of the overflow of the heart that the mouth speaks.

DISCUSSION QUESTIONS

1. If God gave us words that we might glorify Him through them, are my words bringing glory to Him?

2. If our words have great power to bring harm or healing to others, how are my words bringing harm or healing?

3. If our words reveal what is going on in our hearts, what is going on in my heart right now?

CHAPTER TWO

when our words
go BAD

Have you ever thought about how small your tongue is compared to the rest of your body? The average human tongue is only 10 centimeters long, yet what damage can be done with the tongue! Tony Evans has a great illustration for this. He writes, "The Space Shuttle Challenger blew up in 1986 because some little rubber rings weren't correctly placed. They were loose. Lives were lost and destroyed because of a very little thing. Similarly, how much damage have we done or has been done to us because somebody's tongue got loose?"[2]

Evans is right. Though small, our tongue can do great damage.

The reality is that every one of us struggle at times to keep our tongues, our words under control. We can struggle to speak words of wisdom and not foolishness, to speak words of love and not criticism and judgment. We've each brought life and encouragement to others through our words, yet we have also brought pain and hurt. In light of this, we are going to spend the next two chapters considering each of these categories, identifying four types of speech that bring harm and discouragement to others, followed by four types of speech that bring life and build others up. Let's begin by zeroing in on some ways we can cause a lot of damage with our words if we aren't careful.

#1. WORDS OF DECEITFUL FLATTERY

What exactly is flattery? We don't talk about it very much in our culture and yet it can be found all over the place. Simply put, flattery is excessive and insincere praise spoken with deceitful motives. If flattery could speak, it would describe itself this way, *"I don't actually*

*mean the nice, complimentary things I say to you. I say
them because I want something from you. I figure if I
praise you enough, I might get what I want. Don't be
fooled, my motives are not pure. Not for a second."*

Proverbs 29:5 says, "A man who flatters his
neighbor spreads a net for his feet." The literal image
here is using flattering words to draw someone into a
trap in order to prey on them or use them for one's own
purposes. We probably all know or have known a
flatterer. Perhaps you struggle with speaking words of
flattery yourself. Perhaps you don't. But at some point
you could. It can be sneaky. This is why we must be on
guard.

It should be noted that on the surface, words of
flattery and words of encouragement often sound the
same. This is why it can be difficult at times to discern
between the two. However, at the heart of each lies a
major difference. The major difference is that of
motive. If we say something to another person that will
ultimately benefit ourselves, it is flattery. If we speak for
the ultimate benefit and building up of another person,
this is the mark of true, godly encouragement. Motive is
the difference. And a huge difference it is. You see,

while a flatterer seeks his own benefit, the heart of the encourager says, *"I don't want anything from you. I just want to build you up. I want to help you see the amazing ways God is working in and through your life."*

But let us offer a warning at this point. As you grow as an encourager, you may be accused of being a flatterer. It is sad but true. There are so few encouragers in our world that when one comes around, people look at them funny. The same will be true of you. Others will question your motives and look at you suspiciously as if to ask, *"What is this guy up to?"* While we hate to say it, there is good reason for people to feel this way. The disturbing reality is that so often times what appears to be encouragement in our world is not encouragement; it's flattery. But friend, don't let this discourage you! Don't allow Satan to ruin the gift of encouragement you have been called by God to bring to others. Be who you are in Christ and allow the overflow of your love for God and others spill out as words of genuine, life-changing encouragement.

#2. WORDS OF SLANDER AND GOSSIP

Can you think of a time when you've been wounded by gossip or slander? When someone said something about you that wasn't true? Or, perhaps someone said something that was true but was not meant to be shared with anyone else? Words of slander and gossip hurt. They hurt bad. They cut deep. For some of us, the slander or gossip of others from years ago continues to negatively impact our lives to this very day.

Now, while each of us has been personally wounded by the slander and gossip of others, my guess is that you can think of a time when *you* slandered or gossiped, and someone else got wounded. While ashamed to admit it, we both know there have been times in our lives when we have failed in this area. Times when we foolishly hurt others through either speaking words of gossip and slander or failing to put a stop to it when we heard it coming from someone else.

In Scripture, slander and gossip go together, hand in hand. Let us briefly define the two. Slander is the utterance of false charges or misrepresentations which defame and damage another's reputation. Saying things that are not true in order to hurt another person. Slander exists for the purpose of making somebody look bad. At the heart of slander is actual deceit and lies. Slander is untrue.

Gossip is a little different. Gossip is revealing personal or intimate facts about another person to ruin their reputation or make that person look foolish in the eyes of others. Gossip can almost be more painful than slander because while slander often comes from people who don't know you, gossip typically arises from those who are closest to you. Gossip is sharing things that shouldn't be shared. This is why it is so painful. Generally speaking, friends tend to fall into gossip about other friends, whereas enemies often times fall into slander against those they seek to ruin and destroy.

Throughout Scripture, God gives some of his most harsh rebukes to those who slander and gossip. He despises these sins of the tongue. You see, when we slander and gossip, we tear down those created in the very image of God in an ungodly, sinful manner. God hates this. It is offensive to Him. It's the opposite of displaying love. Consider these verses,

Lying lips are an abomination to the Lord, but those who act faithfully are his delight. - Proverbs 12:22

You shall not go around as a slanderer among your people, and you shall not stand up against the life of your neighbor: I am the Lord. - Leviticus 19:16

There are six things that the Lord hates, seven that are an abomination to him: haughty eyes, a lying tongue, and hands that shed innocent blood, a heart that devises wicked plans, feet that make haste to run to evil, a false witness who breathes out lies, and one who sows discord among brothers. - Proverbs 6:16-19

I tell you, on the day of judgment people will give account for every careless word they speak…
- Jesus in Matthew 12:36

The Bible is clear; God despises slander and gossip. The question is, do we despise them as well? One of our favorite authors, Jerry Bridges, wrote a book several years ago called *Respectable Sins*. In this book, he essentially addresses different types of sins that are somewhat "respectable" to most Christians in our day. Meaning, these are sins that are often viewed as minor sins, sins that are not serious enough to be confronted and dealt with in the same way as more serious sins. Respectable sins are sins we typically don't really address within the walls of the church. Knowingly or unknowingly, we just let them slide.

As Bridges describes, there are *big* sins that of course we as Christians deal with quickly and unapologetically. The problem is, in the eyes of God, in light of His holiness, these "respectable sins" are just as evil. Yet for some reason we're comfortable with these. We aren't bothered by them. Why is this? One of the primary reasons is because most of us are guilty of them. We are living with these sins, and we don't have a problem with them. Not really. We have become desensitized to them.

Two of these "respectable sins" are slander and gossip. Because these sins are so prominent in our culture, and so prominent in our churches, we are oblivious to their seriousness. We are oblivious to the ways in which they are an offense to God Himself.

Proverbs 18:7 says,

A fool's mouth is his ruin, and his lips are a snare to his soul.

Ruin. Snare. These words are weighty. They should put some fear into us. To think that our hearts could become desensitized to the seriousness of slander and gossip? That slander and gossip could become so acceptable to us and to those around us that we are virtually numb to them? This is a scary thought. How dangerous to our souls!

Consider what Proverbs 6:12-14 says about slander and gossip. This passage tells us that an ungodly person "goes about with crooked speech, winks with his eyes, signals with his feet, points with his finger, with perverted heart devises evil, continually sowing discord." It's a pretty accurate picture. It's pretty harsh. Continually sowing discord, division, confusion through crooked speech, this is a perfect recipe for bringing dissension to the body of Christ.

Satan loves this.

Some people love it too.

And sometimes, sadly, those people are you and me.

So, the practical question then is, how do we fight against gossip and slander? Or put another way, how do we apply Spirit-empowered wisdom and self-control to this area where many of us struggle? Let us offer three biblical strategies that will hopefully be of help. They come in the form of three specific questions we must be prepared to ask when the temptation to gossip or slander arises.

Question #1. Does this information involve me or affect me directly?

If not, let the chain of gossip end with you. If so, discuss the matter only with the people directly involved. That's just biblical. In Matthew 18, Jesus is very clear that we should go to our Christian brother or sister individually and address this. If it's a situation in which the person refuses to cooperate, then perhaps bringing another Christian with you is appropriate. The bottom line is this: don't be the fire starter that gets—or keeps—this thing going. Because it can spread fast.

Question #2. What is the motive of the person who passed this information on to me?

Be wise! This might be somebody you love deeply, but you know they struggle with sharing things they shouldn't. If this is the case, remember that as much as you care about this individual, you are accountable for yourself and how you respond to these situations. So, how should you respond?.

First, if the motive is clearly not marked by genuine, Christ-like care and concern, you should either lovingly bring correction to the person, or remove yourself from the conversation entirely. On the other hand, if the motive is misguided love (you know they mean well, but this probably isn't the best way to handle things), offer to facilitate a constructive conversation between the person gossiping and the other individual. You might say, *"Let's go talk to that person instead of going to anyone else. We don't need to bring others into this. Let's deal with this directly. That is the most loving thing to do."* This kind of response takes a courageous leader, and you need to be that leader in these situations. Sure, it's easier not to step up, which is why most people don't. It is a bit awkward—especially if you're concerned this person is going to think you're trying to be "holier than thou" and feel judged by you. We don't want anyone to feel this way. But at the end of the day, it doesn't ultimately matter how they "feel." If you are trying to do the right thing, the biblical thing, with kindness and humility, that is what matters most. This is true love in action.

Question #3. What is going on in my heart?

As we've discussed, gossip and slander is a heart issue at the root. This means that if we are tempted ourselves to pass on true or false information about another person, we must be prepared to honestly ask, *"Lord, what is going on in my heart right now? Why am I tempted to gossip about and/or slander this person? What is the root issue here? My pride? My ego? My desire to get revenge? My hunger for other people's approval? Lord, what is going on in my heart?"* As Christians who have the Holy Spirit dwelling within us, we must exercise humility before the Lord in these moments. We must be ready and willing to say with the Psalmist in Psalm 139:23-24,

> Search me, God, and know my heart; test me and know my anxious thoughts.
>
> See if there is any offensive way in me, and lead me in the way everlasting.

So, these are three practical questions that can help us in the battle against gossip and slander. As is the case

with our battle against other sins, we must be proactive
rather than reactive in how we address slander and
gossip in our lives. We need to stay alert. We need to be
prepared, thinking ahead.

#3. WORDS OF ANGER AND ARGUMENT

Don't get us wrong. We are all for good, healthy,
helpful, constructive confrontation and disagreement
with others. But that's not what we have in mind here.
Here we're talking about unhelpful arguments that
result from a negative, angry heart that loves to fight
and argue. A heart that enjoys putting others "in their
place."

Are you an angry person?

What would those closest to you say?

This is an important question we need to ask
ourselves: Am I angry? And if I am angry, why am I
angry? What's going on in my heart that I tend to get
angry so easily? Anger is one of those things that can
just sit in people.

And fester.

And fester some more.

And what happens over time is that you become the type of person—though you don't see this yourself—that people are always walking on eggshells around you. People don't want to get too close to you because it's like they're waiting for a bomb to go off. You don't want to be that person, do you? This is why we need the Lord to help us work through some stuff.

Some hurt. Some regret. Some jealousy. Some bitterness. Whatever it might be, we need the Lord to bring healing to our angry hearts.

You see, when Proverbs talks about a person who stirs up strife (Proverbs 29:22), it is speaking of someone who enjoys stirring the pot. Catch that? They enjoy it. It is amusing to them. Do you know somebody who loves to play "devil's advocate?" I mean, really enjoys it? Would you throw yourself into this camp? What would others say?

Of course, we need people who are critical thinkers. We need people who challenge ideas and seek to sharpen others through helpful critique or disagreement. But there's a big difference between a good, helpful critical thinker and someone who just wants to be critical. One seeks to help people grow, while the other seeks to bring people down. One is a blessing, the other is a burden. God loves one and He despises the other. Listen to what God's Word says about this,

> "A man of wrath stirs up strife, and one given to anger causes much transgression."
> - Proverbs 29:22

> "Make no friendship with a man given to anger, nor go with a wrathful [or hot-tempered] man, lest you learn his ways and entangle yourself in a snare."
> - Proverbs 22:24-25

The image here for "wrathful" or "hot-tempered" is a pot of boiling poison. This type of person responds to practically every negative experience with venom because he or she remains angry with everyone and everything. The reason they're angry is because of issues in their heart. Different kinds of wounds, hurts, and sin that has never been dealt with properly. And that pot of boiling poison is ready to explode at any moment.

Notice the word of warning in Proverbs 22 above. Because anger and argument and cynicism and criticism follow this person like a dark cloud, we must be careful. As verse 25 tells us, if we hang out with this kind of person for too long, we will soon become like him or her ("lest you learn his ways and entangle yourself in a snare."). This is true. The more we hang around angry, critical people, the easier it is for us to become angry and critical. The easier it is to catch the poison.

Of course, the same is true when it comes to encouragement and being an encouraging person. Encouragement is more caught than taught. When you're around encouraging people and watch them loving others and building others up, you're drawn to it, and you catch it.

But we must be on our guard.

We've each seen people who were joyful, encouraging, life-giving individuals, who started hanging out with negative people, and they literally become a different person. Their demeanor changes. Their body language is different. Their tone of voice is no longer joyful and sweet, but angry and hard. This is a reminder for us all. Who we hang out with matters. Who we allow to influence us will shape both our hearts and our behaviors. We are no different than children in this way. That's what we see here in Proverbs 22. The bottom line is that anger must not be given a place to lodge in our hearts. It must not take up residence and reign within us. If anger takes root in our hearts, our words will quickly become weapons that tear down and destroy others.

HOW TO RIGHTLY DEAL WITH OUR ANGER

David Powlison offers helpful insight and counsel on how to control our words of anger in his excellent article, "Dealing with your Anger." In this article, he encourages us to look at our hearts and to humbly pray through five specific questions, asking the Lord to give us wisdom and insight into our anger and how best to deal with it.[3]

#1: What is happening around me when I get angry?

What pushes your buttons? Think of specific times when you become angry. When did you get angry at something that doesn't really matter in God's world? When did you get angry because you had made a good thing more important than God? And, when did you get angry because you were truly wronged?

#2. How do I act when I get angry?

Do you express your anger in *bitterness* (stuffing your anger)? In *arguing* (in expressing your anger freely to those around you)? In *slander* (gossiping and talking about those who have wronged you)? Or in some combination of all three?

Are there any times when anger actually was an expression of love, not hate, and was expressed constructively?

#3. What were my expectations (what did I want, need, demand) when I became angry?

Examining your motives brings God into the discussion, because it reveals what hijacked God's place in your heart. Your answer will show you where you need God's help the most. This will take your focus off the circumstances that were the occasion for your anger and help you to think about why you believed you had a right to be angry *and* had a right to express your anger in the way you did

#4. What message does God have for me, in His word, that will speak to my anger?

We get sinfully angry when we forget that God, not us, is in charge of the world. If you remember that this is God's kingdom and not yours, the way you deal with your anger will be hugely affected. When you add to that an understanding of your real sins, then you will also see how God, in Christ, is tender-hearted and forgiving to you. Your anger will be transformed.

Remembering the height, the depth, the width, and the length of God's love and mercy toward you will put your circumstances and your angry response in the right perspective. Meditating on your need for mercy and God's forgiveness will remind you that no matter what is making you angry, it's so much less than what you have been given in Christ.

Turn to the God who loves you and tell Him all about what is making you angry. Name your suffering, your expectations, your desires, your sins, and all the evil you see and do, and bring yourself to the One who suffered and died for you.

#5. What am I called to do?

Your relationship with God will always lead you to your relationship with people. If you have gone through all these questions, then you don't need a prescription that says, "Do A, B, and C." Because you are in relationship with a living Person, there will be a living quality to your wisdom.

No one can write the script for you on how to deal with your anger. But every time you notice that you are angry, go through these questions. Then remind yourself of God's message of love and mercy to you. As you keep going to Jesus with everything in your heart, you will notice that, step by small step, real change is happening.

Your willingness to be mastered by Jesus and to make following Him your first priority will allow you to imitate Him in expressing your anger in a redemptive way. Then your conflicts won't end with slammed doors and hurt silences. Instead there will be a constructive back-and-forth dialogue that is colored by mercy and a desire for each of you to grow in God's image. Your real, living relationship with the God who loves you to the utmost will allow you to grow in having real human relationships where the conflicts you have will become an opportunity for growth, understanding, and expressing the fruits of the Spirit.

#4. WORDS OF SELF-PROMOTION AND BOASTING

"Do not boast about tomorrow, for you do not know what a day may bring. Let another praise you, and not your own mouth; a stranger, and not your own lips." - Proverbs 27:1-2

Self-promotion and boasting. This is another kind of foolish, ungodly speech that the Bible speaks of. Another "respectable" sin that finds a home in many churches just as it does in our culture at large. This type of speech is often not just accepted but celebrated!

Arrogance and cockiness. Many people are attracted to it, but God is repulsed by it. That's the bottom line.

On a basic level when we talk about self-promotion and boasting, we're identifying that kind of speech that elevates oneself above others, to a superior position or status. This kind of boasting or bragging most often occurs when we intentionally speak highly of ourselves and our accomplishments in order to receive praise and recognition from others.

For many of us, when we think about a self-promoter or a braggart (a great old school word right there!), we probably think of individuals who are known for being cocky. We might think of a particular pro athlete or celebrity who has no problem saying to the world, *"Check me out! Look what I've done! No one can top me!"* This type of boasting is easy to identify. It reeks of self-absorption and is the opposite of humility or meekness.

However, there is a more subtle form of self-promotion and boasting that can be just as, if not more, dangerous. It takes the form of what might be called, false humility, or the "humble brag." False humility sounds like this,

> "I'm not a big deal (but please, tell me that I am)…"

> "I'm not very good at that (but you know as well as I do that I actually am)…"

> "I don't want anyone to notice the nice things I do to serve other people (but I will do all that I can to make sure everyone DOES notice)…"

False humility is sinful. It is ugly. It seeks to steal glory from God. It is often incredibly subtle, but it is self-promotion and boasting to the highest degree.

The reality is that self-promotion and boasting, in whatever form it takes, is really a symptom of a deeper problem that the Bible refers to as pride. That's the real issue. Our prideful hearts. We want attention, and we love to take center stage. The problem is that God alone deserves to be on center stage. He is the hero, not us. And because of this, the Lord considers our self-exaltation and pride a personal offense. In fact, in Proverbs 6, the Lord places a prideful, superior attitude at the head of a list of sins that he hates—a list that includes lying, murder, rebellion, and slander. As Proverbs 16:18 warns, "Pride goes before destruction, and a haughty spirit before a fall."

Friends, our prideful boasting will bring us down. It will. In time, it will. God alone deserves the glory and praise. For this reason, may we boast in God and God alone. The greatest freedom and joy is found not when you are made much of, but when you make much out of God. Praising Him and worshiping Him *is* where the greatest delight is found. There is so much more joy in shining the spotlight on the Lord, where it really belongs, than on ourselves. Having the spotlight on yourself may make you feel good for a moment, but it will always sit empty with you. You know why? Because the spotlight should never be on you. And you know it. It should forever be on the Giver of all good gifts who alone deserves all our praise, all our promotion, and all our boasting!

MOVING ON TO BETTER WORDS

Words of deceitful flattery. Words of slander and gossip. Words of anger and argument. Words of self-promotion and boasting.

These are examples of hurtful, discouraging speech that we see spoken of throughout Scripture. Each of these not only has the potential to do great damage to other people, but each is an offense to our holy God. Again, the Lord did not give us the gift of words to discourage and destroy, He gave them that we might encourage and build up. To this we now turn.

DISCUSSION QUESTIONS

1. Why does our culture seem to so readily gravitate toward damaging speech?

2. In what ways do you personally struggle with using hurtful words?

3. Of the four types of damaging speech listed in this chapter, which one do you struggle with the most? How can you begin to combat this?

CHAPTER 3

the words we were made to SPEAK

Do you ever just stop and think about how amazing the Lord is? How *powerful* He is? How *holy* He is? How *merciful* He is? How *patient* He is? It truly is breathtaking to think about the many attributes of our awesome God.

When it comes to the topic of our words and communication, it is hard not to reflect, in particular, on the attribute of God's creativity. Just think about it for a moment. God didn't have to create human beings with mouths, lips, and a tongue, but He did.

Mouths that can enjoy all kinds of amazing foods and flavors. Mouths that allow us to smile as an expression of joy and thankfulness. Mouths that can produce beautiful music through singing. Mouths that can speak words.

We were created very purposely with the ability to communicate to God and others through words. It is absolutely genius if you think about it. Only our creative God could come up with such an idea. But not only did the Lord in His power and wisdom create us with the ability to communicate with words, He also made us to speak in a certain kind of way with certain types of words.

In the last chapter we considered some of the ways, in our sin, we misuse our words. Ways in which our words can go bad. But for the Christian, we understand that Jesus has saved us and filled us with the Holy Spirit that we might speak in the right way, with the words God wants us to speak. This doesn't mean we speak perfectly, in fact we all stumble in many ways when it comes to the tongue. But it does mean that we should be growing in this area, acknowledging Christ is King over our mouths. That means He is the boss over what does and doesn't come out of them.

I love how pastor and author J.A. Medders puts it,

Jesus is Lord over all. And as the Cosmic Emperor, he reigns over Neptune, pinwheel galaxies, birds, blades of grass, and our words.

Jesus is Lord over our sentences.

The Lordship of Christ has no boundaries. There is not an area of our lives that we can rope off and tell Jesus, "Not here, bub."

Jesus cares about our speech.

Jesus cares about *what* we say.

Jesus cares about *when* we say it.

Jesus cares about *how* we say it.

Jesus cares about *why* we say it.[4]

So, what does it look like to use our words in ways that are pleasing to God? Ways that Jesus wants us to use them? Ways that benefit those around us? Ways that are helpful and build others up? In this chapter, let's consider four specific ways we can honor the Lord and bring life to others through what we say.

#1. WORDS OF WISE COUNSEL AND SOUND ADVICE

Every one of us has received wise counsel at some point in our lives, and it is safe to say that few things are more practically helpful. Can you think of a time when you received really good counsel? Perhaps you were at a point in your life when you were confused and had no idea which way you needed to go. Maybe you were broken and tired and wounded, and you had godly individuals come around you who really wanted the best for you—what God wanted for you. And whether it was what you wanted to hear or not, they spoke wise words to you. Have you been that person for someone else? My guess is you have. The truth is we need these types of people in our life, and we need to be those types of people for others.

God's Word is clear that we need the wise counsel and sound advice that comes from other people,

> "The lips of the wise spread knowledge; not so the hearts of fools." - Proverbs 15:7

> "Without counsel plans fail, but with many advisers they succeed." - Proverbs 15:22

Of course, the key here is not receiving the counsel and advice of the world, or those who are worldly, but rather that which accords with the Word, according to God Himself. James speaks of this as the difference between earthly and heavenly wisdom when he writes,

> Who is wise and understanding among you? Let them show it by their good life, by deeds done in the humility that comes from wisdom. But if you harbor bitter envy and selfish ambition in your hearts, do not boast about it or deny the truth. Such "wisdom" does not come down from heaven but is earthly, unspiritual, demonic. For where you have envy and selfish ambition, there you find disorder and every evil practice. But the wisdom that comes from heaven is first of all pure; then peace-loving,considerate, submissive, full of mercy and good fruit, impartial and sincere. - James 3:13-17

This is why the (capital "C") Church is so important. We need the Church. The Church is the body of Christ. And while God's people, as the Church, are spread out all over the world, we each need to be committed to a local (lower case "c") church. A local congregation. A local body of believers. This is not optional for the biblical Christian. You see, it is in the local church that we learn to love and forgive. It's where we're fed the Word of God and equipped to feed others that same Word. It is where we learn to pray for others, serve others, care for others. It's where we get to take the Lord's supper together with our brothers and sisters in Christ. It's where we learn to encourage and receive encouragement. It's where we both give and receive words of wise counsel and sound advice. This is the church, and what a gift it is!

It is so important to remember that the Church is made up of people Jesus died to save and redeem, and He's putting us together one piece at a time. Yes, we're a mess. We're a bunch of broken people. But we're a body, and we need each other. We need to love each other through good and bad. That's why commitment to a local congregation is so important. Sadly, we live in a day where for many of us, the only thing we are truly committed to is being noncommittal. But if we are truly in Christ, we will see that every faithful local church serves as a type of laboratory that God uses to sanctify us and make us holy for His glory. And as He is doing this work in us, He surrounds us with individuals to help guide us and spur us on through words of wise counsel and sound advice. The Lord calls us to offer the same to others on this same journey.

#2. WORDS OF REPROOF AND CORRECTION

A fool despises his father's instruction, but whoever heeds reproof is prudent.
- Proverbs 15:5

The ear that listens to life-giving reproof will dwell among the wise. Whoever ignores instruction despises himself,   but he who listens to reproof gains intelligence.
- Proverbs 15:31-32

Can you think of a time when someone wisely yet firmly confronted you on your behavior, your thinking, or your attitude, and you grew because of it? We both have. Many times. The Bible refers to this as reproof or correction. This word, reproof, can put some fear into us, can't it? Yet, according to Scripture we all need it to help us continue to grow in godliness.

Proverbs 27:6 reminds us, *"Faithful are the wounds of a friend, but deceitful are the kisses of an enemy."* This is true. And this truth is something we must be mindful of when it comes to giving and receiving words of reproof and correction. Notice four important things that we see in this short verse:

1. The one who does the reproving is someone who **loves the person** he or she corrects. They are a friend.

2. Being corrected by a friend hurts, but like medicine on a wound, **it is good for us** and ultimately brings healing.

3. Friendship should allow **freedom to offer** reproof and helpful, constructive criticism.

4. Not all compliments (or words) are offered with **the right motive.** Flattery is the language of an enemy, not a friend.

When it comes to this matter of reproof, you can see that discernment and discretion is vitally important. There is a right way, a right time, and a right motive for reproving someone that we love. This takes great wisdom. Before we take the initiative to speak words of correction to someone, let us be mindful of these five marks of a God-honoring, loving reproof:

5 Marks of a God-Honoring, Loving Reproof

1.   The motive is to help the other person, not hurt them.

2.   The timing is right.

3.   The reproof is done privately.

4.   The focus is on a specific issue with the hope of growth and improvement.

5.   The reproof is preceded and followed by ongoing affirmation and encouragement.

Chuck Swindoll says this, and we agree with him:

A safe ratio between words of encouragement and words of correction should be around 10 to 1, encouragement to correction. In other words, when you're dealing with other people, whether it's your spouse or your kids or an employee or a friend at church, we should seek to consistently speak words of loving encouragement to them so that when we must share a hard word, that individual knows it comes from a place of deep care and concern, not anger and judgment.

#3. WORDS OF JOYFUL HUMOR

God created laughter. Don't you love that? He made us in such a way that we can laugh at things. And laugh hard! He gave us a sense of humor. As the Giver of laughter, the Lord loves it when we laugh. In fact, one of the things we as Christians should look forward to is laughing with Jesus in heaven. Can you imagine how great His laugh is? Can you imagine? It brings a smile just thinking about it.

Proverbs 17:22 says, "A joyful heart is good medicine." How true this is. We don't know about you, but one of the greatest balms to our hearts when we are weary and discouraged is the joy that comes from laughter. What is so sad is that the world, the flesh, and the devil has hijacked God's gift of humor. Instead of serving as a way to encourage others and build others up, humor in our fallen world is often used to do just the opposite. Humor is used to tear others down, making others look stupid. Or to lead people to indulge in sexual perversion. This was never God's design as the Giver of humor. As Jon Bloom writes,

Humor (like sex) is not a result of the fall. Only perverted humor is. Humor springs from God and, being supreme in all things good, he's the most humorous person in existence. He is the happy God (1 Timothy 1:11), the source of all that is healthy and wholesome and purely hilarious. Anyone who would come up with the ideas to create dogs, llamas, parrots, and proboscis monkeys has a riotous sense of humor.

Preeminent in all things (Colossians 1:18), nobody laughs like God does. He laughs for joy and he laughs in derision at fools who think they can overthrow him (Psalm 2:4). The only reason we have the capacity to laugh ourselves to tears is because we're like him. God is holy. But if we think holiness and humor are incompatible, it's only because we've been sold a diabolical lie.[5]

Proverbs 15:15 reminds us that "*All the days of the afflicted are evil, but the cheerful of heart has a continual feast.*" We say this out of love for you: If you are someone who has to be serious all the time and struggles to laugh at the many goofy situations and circumstances we face in life, then you will become a joy sucker rather than a joy giver. You will suck the joy and laughter right out of people, rather than fueling the joy and laughter they desperately need.

As Christians, as those created in the image of the happy God, we were not made to be so uptight and serious about everything. In fact, because laughter, humor, and joy are all reflections of God Himself, there is something seriously wrong with our hearts if these do not mark our lives as well. Don't get us wrong, there are times when seriousness and sober-mindedness is most appropriate. No question. However, we would argue that even in the midst of the trials that come our way in life, there is much to laugh about. Much to find humor in. As we experience more and more of the grace and kindness of God, may the joy of the Lord overflow into words of singing and laughter and praise!

#4: WORDS OF ENCOURAGEMENT

What exactly is encouragement? When we speak of encouragement, we are talking about sincere expressions of affirmation and gratitude given honestly to another individual in order to build them up. It is helping others see evidences of God's work of grace in their lives. To encourage someone means, quite literally, to "fuel their courage" to be who God made them to be and to live as God made them to live. According to Scripture, a mark of a mature, godly, others focused individual is the practice of regular, consistent, genuine encouragement.

Your spouse needs encouragement.

Your children need encouragement.

Your friends need encouragement.

Your neighbors need encouragement.

Your coworkers need encouragement.

Every person you know is in need of encouragement.

Author and professor Jerry Sittser, writing about the importance of encouraging our brothers and sisters in Christ, says,

> Encouragement is to people in the church what maintenance is to cars and trucks. We have to encourage people to help keep them going as disciples of Jesus over the long haul. When our brothers and sisters in Christ are lacking in zeal and passion, when they lose heart, when they're discouraged and facing disappointment, we must come alongside them with words of encouragement.[6]

I love this description. It is so true. Encouragement is the maintenance ministry of a church. And friends, churches are in need of constant maintenance!

TWO IMPORTANT QUESTIONS WE MUST ASK

Before we speak encouraging words, we must think through two basic and simple questions:

#1. Who needs to be encouraged in my life, right now?

When God brings someone to mind who needs encouraged, we must be prepared to act on it right then. Send them a text and encourage them. Make the call and express encouragement with your words. Write the person a note. It may feel strange. That's ok! Be reminded that God is honored as you encourage. Perhaps you may worry about what to say. But, don't let worry keep you from stepping out and saying the words. It isn't about sharing "the perfect words". Only God has the perfect words. But in His kindness, He will use even your messy and uncomfortable efforts to lovingly build others up who need it!

#2. Throughout the course of my day, am I looking for those who could use some encouragement?

People in need of encouragement are everywhere! When you see them, walk up to them and prayerfully encourage them. It can be something as simple as, "I'm so glad to see you! How have you been?" or, "Hey my friend! Great to see you. How's life?" Or it might be more appropriate to say something deeper, depending on the situation, like, "I see God at work in you. His kindness...His love...His joy really shines through you." So keep your eyes open! Through Christ who gives you strength, step out and encourage!

There are few things greater than receiving genuine words of encouragement, would you agree? Likewise, one of life's greatest joys is in speaking words of encouragement to others. Listen to these Proverbs,

> Anxiety in a man's heart weighs him down, but a good word makes him glad. - Proverbs 12:25

> Gracious words are like a honeycomb, sweetness to the soul and health to the body.
> - Proverbs 16:24

What a gift that through our words we get to lift the weight off a person. That we get to bring sweetness to a person's soul, health to a person's body. Words of encouragement are powerful! People need them and God made us to give them. In 1 Thessalonians 5:11, the Apostle Paul both instructs and encourages the believers in Thessalonica when he says, "Therefore encourage one another and build one another up, just as you are doing." Paul was an encourager! And one of his great desires was to see Christians grow as encouragers themselves.

In Ephesians 4:29, Paul again addresses the importance of speaking words of encouragement, writing,

> Let no corrupting talk come out of your mouths, but only such as is good for building up, as fits the occasion, that it may give grace to those who hear.

There are three main points that Paul makes in this verse—three characteristics of encouraging speech. We are simply calling these, "3 Encouragement Keys." Let's briefly consider each of them.

Key #1: Get rid of words that are corrupt.

This is where Paul starts in verse 29. He says: *"Let no corrupting talk come out of your mouths."* This word for "corrupting" is a forceful word in the Greek. It's the word, *sapros. Sapros* is used in Matthew 13 to describe rotten fish. Can you smell them right now? Putrid, rancid, sick, nasty fish. That's the word Paul uses for "corrupting" here. He is saying we must get rid of words, of language that smells like nasty, rotting fish.

While we looked at several of these in detail in the last chapter, let me briefly list several types of corrupting talk that Paul has is mind:

- words that tear others down

- words of fault-finding and unfair criticism

- words that manipulate others, such as flattery

- words that intentionally hurt and cause pain to others

- words that are false

- words that are mean spirited such as gossip and slander

These are all words we must get rid of, according to Paul. They are rancid and stink like rotten fish!

Key #2: Speak words that intentionally build others up.

We see in the second part of verse 29 that Christians are not only supposed to stop saying bad things, but they are to intentionally say good things, right things, namely, encouraging things. Things that build others up. For the Christian who gets this, it is a great joy! It's like Christmas every day! We "get" to give gifts constantly to others, gifts of encouragement.

Notice Paul says, *"Let no corrupting talk come out of your mouths, but only such as is good for building up as fits the occasion."* In other words, we must seek to build others up wisely and in an appropriate manner. This is what Paul means by "words that fit the occasion." These are words that speak directly and helpfully to an individual at the right time, in the right place, in the right way.

The word here for "building up" in verse 29 is a word that pertains to a person constructing a building or structure of some kind. And so we can imagine that this individual needs to be very careful about selecting and applying the right building materials because the way they're selected, the way they're applied, is vitally connected to the stability of the building, the stability of the structure. And so in the same way, according to Paul, the words we speak should be consistent with the purpose of building others up wisely and effectively.

Key #3: Remember our words are to be vehicles of grace to others.

Look once more at Ephesians 4:29. Paul writes, "Let no corrupting talk come out of your mouths but only such as is good for building up as fits the occasion that it may give grace to those who hear." Paul says that we are to speak words that give grace to those who hear. He's saying this: the Lord desires for our words to be vehicles or channels of His grace. They are to be vehicles or channels of God's love to other people. That is really profound if you think about it.

As mentioned earlier, our words can bring life, or our words can bring death. Our words can lift up, or our words can tear down. Our words can be messengers of grace, or our words can be messengers of judgment. This is huge. And it means this: before we speak, we need to think about what we are about to say. We need to ask ourselves a few questions, three in particular:

1: **What is my motive for speaking?** What is honestly my motive for speaking? What do I hope to accomplish

by opening up my mouth? Are these words necessary? Are these words actually helpful?

#2. What impact will my words have on this person? The words I am about to speak to another person: will they impact them for good or bad? Will they leave feeling more loved by me? Will they feel helped by me? Will my words be a vehicle of grace or a vehicle of pain?

#3. What impact would my words have if they were spoken to ME? I (Mark) grew up attending Verda James Elementary School in Casper, Wyoming. It was a great place to grow up. Every year on the first day of school our principal, Mr. Hambrick, would bring all of us into the gymnasium for our first assembly of the year. You can imagine all of these little bodies sitting down, legs crossed, packing out this little gymnasium. It was quite a sight.

Once all 400 or so of us quieted down, Mr. Hambrick would get up, grab a microphone, and give "The Speech." It was known as "The Speech" because it was the same speech every single year. It went like this,

> "Verda James, I'm so excited you're here! It's going to be another great year. Now you know, here at Verda James we have one rule, just one rule. And if we follow this one rule, oh, we'll have a lot of fun together this year. But if we don't follow this rule, oh, it will be a big problem."

And then he'd say,

> "Here is our one rule: Do unto others as you would have them do unto you."

Sure enough, Mr. Hambrick would remind us of this rule everytime we gathered together in that gym as a student body. I didn't think much of it then, but how genius was this rule. Sounds like something Jesus would say (see Matthew 7:12)!

Imagine if we were mindful of this wisdom before we opened our mouths to speak. If we thought to ourselves, "Before I speak these words, how would I feel if someone spoke the same words to me, in the same way I'm about to speak them?" Asking this question, and then acting accordingly, is a very simple but helpful way to put "do unto others as you would have them do unto you," into practice. This is what it looks like to practice self-control of the tongue. And as a Christian, the Holy Spirit will give you the strength you need to consistently put into practice this kind of self-control, out of love for God and love for others.

OUR WORDS ARE WEIGHTY

As we have seen over and over again in Scripture, our words carry enormous weight—more weight than most of us realize. Our words can impact people for decades, providing the courage to press on or giving them one more reason to give up. We are shaping others through the words we speak. We really are. For this reason, God calls us and equips us to be relentless encouragers of others.

Let's do this. Let's begin to pursue others with relentless encouragement!

DISCUSSION QUESTIONS

1. Think for a moment about a time when someone's words truly helped you. Why were their words so impactful?

2. Of the four types of helpful speech listed in this chapter, what type do you feel you're best at giving? Why do you think this is?

3. How can you grow as one who encourages others?

PART 2:
BECOMING A RELENTLESS ENCOURAGER

CHAPTER FOUR

why EVERYONE
needs encouragement

I (Scott) will never forget a trip to the grocery store with my daughter, Addi, when she was about 8 years old. As we were in line getting ready for our turn at the register to check out, we noticed that the cashier looked weary, like it had perhaps been a long day for her. She didn't seem very excited to be there. Truly, she just looked worn out and ready to go home. My daughter must have perceived this on some level, or maybe she just felt bad for her. I'm not totally sure. But suddenly, with love and boldness, Addi said to the cashier, "God loves you and so do I." There was a moment of silence. I held my breath, not sure how Addi's boldness would be received. To my surprise, the cashier became teary and said, "Thank you so much. I really needed that. That made my day!" The cashier proceeded to come from behind the counter to give Addi a hug before we left.

This simple grocery store encounter is such a good reminder of how people all around us are discouraged, carrying heavy loads, burdened, and in need of an encouraging word. And the good news is that God has saved us and filled us with His Spirit of love that we might be daily messengers of encouraging words to others! This is part of our calling and purpose as believers on this earth; to build up everyone we meet with words that bring life, joy, and hope.

While there are many reasons why those around us need to be encouraged on a regular basis, let's consider nine of the most prominent. The two of us try to remind ourselves of these often as they help fuel both our conviction and practice of encouragement. We recommend you do the same.

#1. LIFE IS HARD.

A great pastor we both used to work with, Deral Schrom, would always say, *"Be kind because everyone you meet is fighting a hard battle."* That's the truth. As pastors, when we get up to preach on Sundays, we must remember that everybody in that room is fighting a hard battle. We all are. We have different battles, different fears, different insecurities. We're broken people, and we need Jesus. We've got to remember that. We have to remember that when we're sitting down with somebody for lunch, they're fighting a hard battle. Even if it appears that they're not, they are. That is life this side of heaven in a broken world.

Life is hard. It just is.

This is why Christ calls us to not add further heaviness and burden to others, but to help lift them! As Paul writes in Galatians 6:2, "Bear one another's burdens, and so fulfill the law of Christ." One of the simplest ways we can do this is through speaking words of encouragement. Everyone we meet needs more encouragement, not less.

#2. THERE IS MUCH TO BE DISCOURAGED ABOUT IN OUR WORLD.

For those we come into contact with on a daily basis, you can safely assume that the majority of them are pretty discouraged by a lot of things. Even if it's not directly related to their own personal life, they're hearing it in the news.

It's everywhere.

Let's be honest, we're not doom and gloom guys but there's a lot to be discouraged about. It is easy for any of us to become consumed with all that is wrong, making it difficult to see what is right, good, and beautiful. Some people are in marriages that are incredibly painful. All they seem to hear from their spouse are words that degrade and discourage them. Some folks work in jobs where they are constantly criticized, never affirmed in the good they are doing for the company or organization. Others run with "friends" who constantly put them down and make them feel like an idiot.

Sadly, we could go on and on.

Regardless of "the front" some people put up, making it seem like all is well and that they have it all together, many people are incredibly discouraged. And because of this, in a world where we are daily bombarded with so many discouraging words, the Lord calls us to shine light into the lives of others through intentional encouragement. This kind of intentional encouragement brings hope to those who are discouraged and feeling hopeless. It brings hope in the Lord. It brings hope in His goodness and in His power. It brings hope that He is alive and at work in amazing ways, bringing about much good in what often feels like a dark and discouraging world.

Encouragement brings hope in the face of discouragement.

#3. WE HAVE AN ENEMY WHO LIES AND DECEIVES.

Satan is real. He's not some made-up, mythological figure. He's an enemy, but he's not someone we need to fear. The Bible refers to our enemy as a deceiver and a liar. So the battle is the mind. This is why we fight lies and deceit with the truth—the truth of the Word, the truth of who we are in Christ, the truth of the Gospel.

When we're bombarded with lies all the time, which we are, many of us don't even recognize when we're being lied to. This is a major problem. This is why many of us live our lives day in and day out believing lies about God, about ourselves, about the world, and about others. In believing so much untruth, it can be like we are living in a story that's not a true story; it's make-believe, but we think it's real. It does not correspond with reality.

This is why we need to encourage others through the speaking of truth. Through "speaking Bible" to them. This is no game. Satan wants to destroy you. And us. And every person we meet. This is why Peter exhorts us, "Be sober-minded; be watchful. Your adversary the devil prowls around like a roaring lion, seeking someone to devour." (1 Peter 5:8) The devil is the ultimate discourager. How does he lie to you? Ever thought about it? It might be, *"Look at you. Look at your body. Look at your face. You're so unattractive."* It could be: *"Man, you are dumb. Everybody's smarter than you."* Or, *"You're terrible at your job."* Or, *"You're a horrible mom."*

Or, *"You call yourself a husband?"* Or, *"You call yourself a pastor? You're a joke!"*

We all get it.

Satan passes no one by.

He is the great discourager.

This is why we must fight for others through encouragement. And it is a fight we must fight. Encouragement is a war against discouragement, against the lies of the enemy, for other people. The question is: Will we do whatever it takes to be speakers of truth, love, and hope to others? Will we fight for them?

Christ saved us and has given us all we need through the power of the Spirit to fight this fight. Let us trust Him in this.

#4. PEOPLE SAY INCREDIBLY HURTFUL, MEAN-SPIRITED THINGS.

It is amazing how hurtful, mean-spirited words can stick. I bet if you stop and think about it right now, you can remember specific times in your life when someone made fun of you or put you down. It may have happened years ago, but the words still hurt.

Awhile back, I (Mark) was visiting with a woman in our church who opened up to me about one of the greatest struggles in her life. At the age of 13, this kind, godly woman was told by a few of her closest middle school friends that her nose was huge and ugly. They said her nose was so unattractive, so hideous, no boy would ever want to date her, let alone marry her someday.

As she grew older, for more than 30 years, all she saw in the mirror was an ugly girl with a huge, disgusting nose. Only in the past few years as she has grown to better understand her identity and ultimate value in Jesus Christ has she begun to experience healing from these verbal wounds from years ago.

I wish these types of stories were few and far between, but they are not. The sad reality is that just like my friend, people all around us carry deep wounds from hurtful, mean-spirited words others have spoken to them in the past. Just one remark can shape a person's entire outlook on life for decades. We can help to counter these insults, put-downs, and straight up lies through intentional words of genuine, loving, honest encouragement.

#5. OUR SHAME AND SENSE OF FAILURE CAN FEEL OVERWHELMING.

We all make mistakes. We all make many mistakes. And the shame and sense of failure that often results from these mistakes can feel overwhelming. Many people are paralyzed by this sense of shame and failure.

This is why encouraging those around us with the truth of the Gospel is so important. Yes, we all make mistakes and we all fall far short of the glory of God. Yet, the Lord Jesus died and was raised on our behalf, taking our shame and failure upon Himself. As Jon Bloom writes,

> There is only one place to hide that offers the protection we seek, where all our shame is covered and we no longer need to fear: the refuge of Jesus Christ (Hebrews 6:18–20). Jesus's death and resurrection is the only remedy for the shame we feel over our grievous sin-failures (Hebrews 9:26). There is nowhere else to go with our sin; there is no other atonement (Acts 4:12). But if we hide in Jesus, he provides us a complete cleansing (1 John 1:9). And when that happens, all God's promises, which find their yes in Christ (2 Corinthians 1:20), become ours if we believe and receive them. And the grace that flows from these

promises to us through faith are all-sufficient and abounding and provide for all our other shameful weaknesses and failures (2 Corinthians 9:8).[7]

This is the good news of the Gospel! This is the amazing grace of God! Sadly, many of us have a really hard time with grace. Many of us have a hard time experiencing it and believing that the grace of God is truly free, covering all of our guilt, all of our shame, and all of our failure. Yet it is true. Not only must we remind ourselves of these glorious truths, we must remind other believers around us as well. There is nothing more encouraging to our souls than hearing the good news of God's love and grace for us in Jesus. Let us be proclaimers of this good news that brings hope and peace to others like nothing else can.

#6. MANY PEOPLE STRUGGLE WITH A DEEP SENSE OF LONELINESS.

All around us are individuals who battle a deep sense of loneliness in their lives. We may not always recognize it, but it is true. Whether it is the result of losing a spouse, or an unexpected move to a new, unfamiliar community, or an ongoing difficulty finding friends they truly connect with, the reality is that many in our world struggle greatly with a sense of profound loneliness.

Sadly, this is often just as true for those inside our churches as it is for those outside. Russell Moore writes,

> The fact that the most "Christianized" places in this country are also among the loneliest should be alarming to us of just how far we have drifted from seeing the biblical picture of the gospel, which balances for us the personal and the communal, the one and the many, the individual and the community. In Christ alone, we are in Christ, together.[8]

So often when an individual is lonely, they feel as though no one notices them. No one needs them. Perhaps, that no one cares. This can absolutely eat a person up inside. If you have ever struggled with loneliness, you know how terrible this feels. This is why one of the most powerful ways we as Christians can help others fight loneliness is by pursuing them with words of encouragement and affirmation. To go to them and speak words of truth. Words that lift them up as they are reminded of their value and worth in the eyes of God.

Relentless encouragers are just that, relentless. And few people need relentless encouragement more than the lonely.

#7. WE ARE IN A DAILY BATTLE AGAINST SIN.

Each day every one of us faces a battle. We aren't always cognizant of the battle, but it's there. That battle is between the Spirit and the flesh. Galatians 5:17 puts it this way, "For the flesh desires what is against the Spirit, and the Spirit desires what is against the flesh; these are opposed to each other, so that you don't do what you want."

This battle is very real. God is at work in us, growing us in the fruit of the Spirit, but our "old nature" resists and fights and wants to do what our sin craves. We all face this. Satan tries to make us think we are the only one struggling with our flesh in whatever way we may struggle. That just isn't true though!

God has given us the privilege of helping one another as we face this real war. God gives us a weapon essential in this battle -- It's called encouragement! John Piper says this about our call to exhort one another everyday:

> You are God's appointed means to keep your brother or sister from falling into sin...This is one of the great callings on your life as a Christian -- all of you. This is the calling of Christian fellowship -- in all its forms.[9]

By God's grace, let's take God's exhortation to us as Christ followers to heart!

> But encourage each other daily, while it is still called today, so that none of you is hardened by sin's deception. - Hebrews 3:13

#8. ANXIETY AND WORRY WEIGH MANY OF US DOWN.

Do you know someone who struggles with worry? Have you encountered anyone who battles with anxiety? Surely you have. The truth is that we know about worry and anxiety all too well. You may have family or friends that fight much with it. In fact, many of us personally grapple with anxiety and worry everyday.

The reality is this, many people battle fear, worry, and anxiety. People at our places of work, at our schools, at restaurants, at our churches, at...everywhere, are often heavy with the burden of anxiety. It's important for us to be increasingly aware of this. Not so we can be hopeless or depressed about it, but rather so we can go to God in prayer for others and for ourselves, and receive the help God wants to give.

God tells us to cast all our anxieties on Him because He cares for us (1 Peter 5:7). God tells us to not worry about anything, but instead to come to Him in prayer with everything (Philippians 4:6). What encouragement these passages bring us! God doesn't want us to carry our worries and anxieties, rather He wants us to bring them to Him who alone can handle them. As relentless encouragers, we must regularly remind one another of this truth, to share a good word with one another in order to lighten the load. Proverbs 12:25 (NLT) puts it this way, "Worry weighs a person down; an encouraging word cheers a person up." May we be used often to encourage one another when worry threatens to weigh us down!

#9. ENCOURAGEMENT IS LOVE IN WORDS, AND WE ALL NEED LOVE.

One of our heroes is Steven Curtis Chapman. He has written many powerful, encouraging songs over the years. His ability to lift people up through his music is one of the reasons why he is loved by so many. One of his great, but lesser known songs is called, "All That's Left". It's a song about when it's all said and done, what really, truly matters is love. The bridge of the song lyrically says, "This is why our hearts are beating. To love each other as we have been loved. Everything else is a fleeting shadow. But love endures all things, believes all things, and hopes all things, love never ends." This song is really just a sweet echo of Scripture about love.

We all need love. We all need to receive it, and we all need to give it away so we can fully mature. Without love, real love that God created, we have nothing. When love is lacking, nothing is really right. In fact, without love all we say, all we believe, and all we do is worthless (1 Corinthians 13:1-3). On the other hand, Jesus said this about loving God with all we are and loving our neighbor as ourselves: "Do this and you will live!" (Luke 10:28)

Love is more than words, but no doubt an important, key way we communicate love is with words. Real encouragement is love communicated with words. Encouragement is speaking with love to help another, to build up another, to remind another that God is for them, with them, that they aren't alone, and that we care.

Encouraging someone is expressing love verbally, and love is to be the main mark for all of us as Christians (John 13:34-35).

PEOPLE NEED ENCOURAGEMENT... WILL WE GIVE IT?

People all around us need encouragement! God wants to graciously use us to encourage. The question is, will we let God use us to build up our neighbor? Will we open our eyes to see God's children all around us who could use a helpful word? Will we speak the words, write the note, send the text, make the call? Will we speak the words of encouragement so many people desperately need to hear?

We pray so.

By God's grace and power, let us seek to relentlessly encourage others, building them up as we point them to the only One who can give them true and lasting encouragement, Christ Jesus Himself.

> "But encourage each other daily, while it is still called today…" (Hebrews 3:13)

DISCUSSION QUESTIONS

1. This chapter lists nine reasons why people need encouragement. Which do you most identify with and why?

2. What are some specific ways you can come alongside and encourage those in your life who are battling anxiety? Guilt and shame? Loneliness? Make a list and then take action.

3. What holds you back from building others up more often?

CHAPTER FIVE

what holds us BACK
from encouraging others

Here is the sad truth: In our world, discouragement is pervasive. Dejection and depression run rampant. We are inundated with voices of pessimism, cynicism, and despair. As Rick Warren put it,

> We live in a deeply negative culture, where put-downs seem to be a favorite form of humor. People are constantly demeaned and degraded...criticized and maligned. When somebody comes along and says, 'Good job!' it makes a tremendous difference.[10]

It is simple, but true. What we readily find in our society is criticism. What is missing and needed is much more encouragement.

So, why do so many of us struggle to encourage others? Why is it so hard for us? We want to be the kinds of Christians that are growing as encouragers, don't we? Sadly, encouragement is not something you hear taught on very often or find many people passionate about. Yet when we look at the Bible and reflect on the call to love our neighbor as ourselves, there are few greater expressions than that of encouragement. As we've discussed earlier in this book, encouragement is love spoken. That's what it is: love spoken. We talk about serving people with our hands, which is critically important, but we rarely talk about serving people with our mouths, with our words.

Why is this?

What holds us back from encouraging others as the Bible commands?

What is keeping us from living our lives as relentless encouragers?

In the last chapter we looked at nine reasons why people need encouragement so badly. In this chapter we will consider nine reasons why we fail to encourage others the way that we should. Which of these are true for you? Which of these are hindering you from encouraging those who need it?

#1. PRIDE

One of the reasons many people don't relentlessly encourage others is pride. Pride in our hearts. Pride that says, "If I build you up with my words, it might cause you and others to think you are better than me in some way. In my heart, I want to be made much of. I want to be noticed. I want to be recognized by others. I want to be encouraged. Encouraging you might interfere with this. So, instead of encouraging you, I will stay silent."

Isn't pride twisted? It is like poison to our souls. And it is not only killing us, but it is hindering the types of loving, encouraging, others-focused relationships Jesus desires for us. The bottom line is that if we are going to grow as relentless encouragers, we must seek to put pride to death. Let's consider three simple strategies to help weaken pride and cultivate humility in our hearts.[11]

#1. Begin your day by acknowledging your dependence upon God and your need for God.

We must choose to submit to God and His Spirit first thing each morning. We must look to Him for strength from the moment we wake up to the moment we go to bed. This daily acknowledgement of our need for God will help grow in us a posture and attitude of humility before the Lord and others.

#2. Reflect on the wonder of the cross.

How often do we stop and simply stand amazed at the cross? How often do we take the time to meditate on key passages dealing with the work of Christ on the cross on our behalf? We *must* do this! This must become a daily discipline if we are to grow as relentless encouragers. Reflecting on the wonder of the cross helps us kill pride that creeps up in our hearts.

#3. Study God and His Word.

As Christians, studying theology should not just be a means of simply filling our minds with knowledge about God. It should fuel the affections of our hearts as we grow more and more amazed by the power, beauty, and faithfulness of God in all things. It should set us on fire to know and love God deeply. It should drive us to our knees in worship, reminding us that He is God and we are not. Studying God and His Word helps to weaken pride and cultivate humility.

As we work to kill pride in our hearts in these ways, the Holy Spirit will grow us as lovers and encouragers of others. Look, if we are quicker to criticize rather than encourage those around us, this is evidence of a heart that is unhealthy. There is pride and insecurity in there. Over time, this will do serious damage to people. We need to be willing to do our own heart work first before our harshness causes great damage to others.

There is so much good that is happening in people's lives! God is at work! But, do we see it? Are we looking for it? Relentless encouragers see the great things God is doing in people's lives and points them out for all to see. In doing this, we get to show God off and give Him glory!

#2. AWKWARDNESS

Awkwardness. There is a lot of awkwardness in life, isn't there? Sammy Rhodes has an excellent description of awkwardness in his great article, "Don't Waste Your Awkwardness." He writes,

> If we had to make our relationship with awkwardness Facebook official, we would probably have to choose the "It's complicated" option. On the one hand, we're drawn to awkwardness. It's in the shows we love: The Office, Arrested Development, Parks and Rec, Modern Family, and New Girl. We can't seem to get enough of awkwardness.
>
> And yet we're terrified of it, especially of being marked with what my friend Les Newsom calls the new scarlet letter: "A" for awkwardness. One of our greatest fears is leaving a party only to have friends lock eyes with each other and complain about how awkward we were.
>
> Maybe we haven't yet realized we're both drawn to awkwardness and afraid of it because deep down we're all awkward people. Just think about the last time you were in an elevator. Everyone's awkwardness shines a little brighter in an elevator.[12]

Let's just name it. Encouraging others can be kind of awkward. It shouldn't be, but it is. In a world where encouragement is so rare, it feels strange for many people. Both to those giving encouragement and those receiving it. Because of this awkwardness, most of us simply don't do it. "It just feels weird," we think to ourselves.

So, what do we do about the awkwardness that comes with encouraging others? We lean into it.

That's right. Lean into the awkward.

For the relentless encourager, instead of allowing the awkwardness of encouragement to mute their words, they lean into the awkward of the moment and encourage anyway.

This must be true of everyone of us. May the Lord give us courage to let our loving encouragement be stronger than our fear of the awkward. Stronger than our fear of what others might think. God will use your encouragement to build up others. Everytime, God will use it. Lean into the awkward. It's worth it.

#3. LAZINESS

Laziness is a common theme throughout the Bible. And it's more than fair to say that the Lord doesn't have favorable things to say about it. For example,

> The soul of the sluggard craves and gets nothing, while the soul of the diligent is richly supplied. - Proverbs 13:4

> Through sloth the roof sinks in, and through indolence the house leaks. - Ecclesiastes 10:18.

> The desire of the sluggard kills him, for his hands refuse to labor. - Proverbs 21:25

Laziness is the cause of much stagnation in the spiritual lives of many Christians. It is also a major hindrance to effective encouragement. The truth of the matter is that some of us don't encourage simply because we're too lazy. Here's what we mean. We can hear teaching or read an article or blog post on encouragement, be reminded of its importance, but then fail to act on what we just read. Because we are too lazy.

For many, it's not a matter of understanding the power of encouragement, it is a matter of not following through on what we know. It takes time and energy and intentionality we choose not to give. While it doesn't take a ton of effort to encourage others, it does take some. Don't let laziness steal the joy and blessing that comes to both the giver and receiver of genuine encouragement.

#4. DISTRACTIONS

We are a distracted people, aren't we? Many of us are so busy, we are just trying to keeps our heads afloat. Our lives feel like they are moving in a hundred different directions all the time! Not to mention the fact that we are bombarded by technological temptations that are constantly stealing our attention and focus.

"Are you using your phone, or is your phone using you? Can you put it down? Can you turn it off?"

These were the blunt rhetorical questions asked by Denzel Washington in a recent interview with BBC television. "I'm not knocking the phone," the actor reiterated. "We have to at least ask ourselves — around the world — what is [the smartphone] doing to us?"[13]

Denzel is right! And it isn't just our phones that are a problem. It is Facebook, and Twitter, and Instagram, and Netflix, and on and on we could go. Now, none of these things are bad in and of themselves. In fact, much good can come from them. However, we must be honest and recognize they are sources of great distraction for most of us. Distraction from the things that matter most, including our encouragement of others.

You might be asking, *"How do our daily distractions have anything to do with encouraging people?"* Here is how. Distractions cause many of us to fail in our *follow through.* Our follow through to actually turn an encouraging thought into an encouraging word. Remember, encouraging thoughts do nothing to build another person up. They must HEAR an encouraging word. We must SPEAK encouragement. This takes follow through. And distractions often hinder our follow through.

Let me (Mark) share a simple example of what I'm talking about. There is a godly woman in our church named Shirley who makes incredible banana bread. I mean, it is seriously incredible. The thought of it right now makes me want to call her and see if she happens to have a loaf sitting on her kitchen counter that I could devour later today. Well, it would be easy for me to think, *"I need to encourage Shirley about her bread! Not just how great it tastes, but more than that, what a blessing she is in baking that bread for those in our church who are hurting and discouraged. She needs to know that God is using her and that banana bread to minister to our congregation!"* Of course, just as I begin to think this encouraging thought, I'm confronted with a host of other things in my day that steal my time and attention.

And what happens?

I get distracted and never follow through on encouraging Shirley. As a result, I miss out on the joy of building up my sister and she misses out on receiving a kind word that will surely encourage her. This kind of thing happens all the time, doesn't it?

Distractions are always coming our way. This is why we must encourage, *now*. Not later. Don't wait.

Make the call. Send the text. Shoot the email. Stop by the house. Speak that encouraging word...now.

#5. FEAR

Communication can be a tricky thing at times. How often have we said something we thought would be helpful or encouraging to someone but somehow they took offense to our words. Our desire was to build this person up but clearly they didn't take it that way for whatever reason.

Ever been there? It doesn't feel good. In fact, it can leave us a bit shocked. More than that, it can instill within us a sense of fear to encourage others in the future. What if they take my words the wrong way? What if instead of feeling encouraged they somehow feel put down or criticized?

While communication can indeed be a tricky thing, and sometimes people will misinterpret our words and motives for speaking, we cannot allow those unfortunate experiences to hinder or limit our practice of relentless encouragement. The reality is that for every one person who responds negatively to our encouragement, there are countless others who will be built up and edified through our words. While we want to be wise in how we communicate, being sensitive to how an individual may receive our words, at the end of the day, we cannot allow fear of others' response dictate our practice of encouragement. The Lord made us to encourage those around us. Let's trust Him to use these words for His purposes in their lives.

#6. SELF-ABSORPTION

Tim Keller wrote a great little book a few years ago entitled, *The Freedom of Self-Forgetfulness.* We highly recommend it. The title perfectly captures the main point Keller is seeking to make. When we seek, by the Spirit, to put to death self-centeredness, self-absorption, and self-obsession, replacing these with Christ-centered self-forgetfulness, it is there that we find true freedom. It is there that we find peace that passes understanding. It is there that we become men and women who are able to truly love God and love others the way Christ calls us to. There really is freedom in self-forgetfulness.

Sadly, it is our self-absorption that often interferes with our ability to encourage others well. Many of us are so focused on ourselves that we simply don't think about others very often, let alone take the time to encourage them. Building others up through our words doesn't even enter our radar. So, what can we do about our self-absorption? How can we move from preoccupation with self to preoccupation with others? The answer: Growing in gospel-humility. Keller writes,

> C.S. Lewis in *Mere Christianity* makes a brilliant observation about gospel-humility at the very end of his chapter on pride. If we were to meet a truly humble person, Lewis says, we would never come away from meeting them thinking they were humble. They would not be always telling us they were a nobody (because a person who keeps saying they are a nobody is actually a self-obsessed person). The thing we would remember from meeting a truly gospel-humble person is how much they seemed to be totally interested in us. Because the essence of gospel-humility is not thinking more of myself or thinking less of myself, it is thinking of myself less.

> Gospel-humility is not needing to think about myself. Not needing to connect things with myself. It is an end to thoughts such as, 'I'm in this room with these people, does that make me look good? Do I want to be here?' True gospel-humility means I stop connecting every experience, every conversation, with myself. In fact, I stop thinking about myself. The freedom of self-forgetfulness. The blessed rest that only self-forgetfulness brings.[14]

As we grow in gospel-humility and self-forgetfulness, we will discover the freedom and joy that comes with loving and encouraging others! As Paul writes in Philippians 2:4, *"Let each of you look not only to his own interests, but also to the interests of others."* May the Lord increasingly make us those who are preoccupied with the interests of others, seeking to build them up however we can.

#7. APATHY

It is difficult to fully measure just how powerful our words of encouragement are. What we know is that for many of us, our lives have in many ways been directed and shaped by words of encouragement that have been spoken to us at different points on our journey.

Just think about the past week or two of your life. Our guess is that at some point in the past few weeks someone said something encouraging to you. Perhaps they called you, or sent you an encouraging text, a Facebook message, or an email, and they shared an encouraging word with you. It made your day, right? Just one little comment. If this is true for you, surely it is true for others as well. Let us never underestimate the power of encouragement.

#8. LOVELESSNESS

The reason some of us don't encourage others is because, quite honestly, we just don't love people very much. And that is a problem for anyone who claims to love and follow Jesus. Remember, encouragement is a fruit of love. It's an expression of love toward other people.

If you are someone who struggles to love other people, and therefore finds it difficult to speak encouraging words to others, our encouragement is to bring this before the Lord. To be honest with Him about the lack of love you feel in your heart toward those around you. This kind of love can only begin when God changes our hearts and fills us with His Spirit to love others. We can't "will" ourselves to become loving people. We must humble ourselves and submit to God, allowing Him to change us from the inside-out. This is what God desires to do in each of us.

Just as God has shown radical, undeserved love toward us through the Gospel, He is at work to transform us into vessels who exude this same love toward others.

#9. FAVORITISM

If we are to be biblical Christians, we must understand that showing favoritism has no place in our hearts or in the way we live our lives. James, the brother of Jesus, had much to say on this topic. Listen to his words in James 2:1-9:

> [1]My brothers, show no partiality as you hold the faith in our Lord Jesus Christ, the Lord of glory. [2]For if a man wearing a gold ring and fine clothing comes into your assembly, and a poor man in shabby clothing also comes in, [3]and if you pay attention to the one who wears the fine clothing and say, "You sit here in a good place," while you say to the poor man, "You stand over there," or, "Sit down at my feet," [4]have you not then made distinctions among yourselves and become judges with evil thoughts? [5]Listen, my beloved brothers, has not God chosen those who are poor in the world to be rich in faith and heirs of the kingdom, which he has promised to those who love him? [6]But you have dishonored the poor man. Are not the rich the ones

who oppress you, and the ones who drag you into court? [7] Are they not the ones who blaspheme the honorable name by which you were called? [8] If you really fulfill the royal law according to the Scripture, "You shall love your neighbor as yourself," you are doing well. [9] But if you show partiality, you are committing sin and are convicted by the law as transgressors.

Simply put, favoritism, or partiality, has no place in the Christian life. This includes who we choose to encourage. We cannot play favorites in this. Sure, there will always be certain people with whom we are really comfortable loving on and encouraging, while there are others that are more difficult. Maybe it is because their personality is different than yours, they have different interests than you do, perhaps they're younger than you or older than you or wear different clothes than you do. Whatever it might be, don't allow your differences to mute your words of encouragement in their life. Don't allow favoritism to creep in and side-track this beautiful expression of God's love and grace. Instead, ask the Lord to help you with this. Ask Him to open your eyes to see those in need of encouragement that you might normally not be drawn to.

MAY NOTHING HOLD US BACK
FROM ENCOURAGING OTHERS

There are plenty of reasons why we don't encourage. But the fact remains, people need encouragement. More importantly, God has both invited and commanded us, as His children, to encourage others. Hebrews 10:23-25 puts it this way, "Let us hold fast the confession of our hope without wavering, for He who promised is faithful. And let us consider how to stir up one another to love and good works, not neglecting to meet together, as is the habit of some, but encouraging one another, and all the more as you see the Day drawing near." Scotty Smith, reflecting on this passage says,

> This awesome passage calls us to be regular and robust in bringing encouragement to friends and family members, co-workers. Encouragement is always important, but in our culture of criticism and cynicism, it's never been more needed.

How true this is!

DISCUSSION QUESTIONS

1. For many of us, giving encouragement doesn't come naturally. Why does it seem so foreign?

2. What's preventing you from growing as a relentless encourager of others?

3. What do you need to personally bring to God in prayer to grow as one who builds up rather than tears down?

CHAPTER SIX

how to PRACTICE
relentless encouragement

It is one thing to understand the importance and power of encouragement, it is quite another to actually put it into practice. In this final chapter, we want to get really practical and consider a number of different ways we can begin to live our daily lives as relentless encouragers. This is the main reason we wrote this book in the first place! To help each of us grow as those who actually practice radical, intentional, relentless encouragement, bringing life to others everyday through what we say. But, before we dive into different strategies and practices, it is critical that we take a few moments to remember and reflect on the one ingredient that makes this kind of encouraging life even possible: The power of God.

RELENTLESS ENCOURAGERS NEED POWER

> "OK, I get it. Encouraging others is really, really important. The truth is, I want to be an encouraging person, but I just don't know if I have it in me."

These words recently came from a young man in our church who had just attended a class I (Mark) was teaching on biblical encouragement. The fact is, my young friend is exactly right. He doesn't have it within himself to become a relentless encourager. And neither do you. Neither do I.

To become relentless encouragers, we need strength that comes from outside of us, from the Lord Himself. Only the Lord can transform us into encouragers through the power of His gospel and the power of the Holy Spirit. Only through Christ can we truly do anything worthwhile and fruitful (Philippians 4:13; John 15:4). So, as we look to Jesus, walk with

Him, and set out to follow His commands, let's consider a few of the ways we find the power to encourage others as we are called to.

#1. We must go to God daily to be encouraged ourselves.

God is the Author and Inventor of encouragement. God is the great Encourager! In Him we find ultimate encouragement through prayer and through the strength He alone provides (Psalm 138:3). Through His Word we find ongoing encouragement during the ups and downs of life. Psalm 119:28 (NLT) says, "I weep with sorrow; encourage me by Your Word." May we always come honestly to God in prayer like this, humble and expectant. May we go to His Word daily to meet with Him, and in so doing, find true, sustaining encouragement for our souls. In God alone do we truly find the comfort, encouragement, and peace we long for (2 Corinthians 7:6; 2 Corinthians 1:3; John 14:27). How important it is that we remember this everyday - go straight to the Lord!

As we go to God in prayer, reading and studying His Word, we are reminded of encouraging truths like,

"The Lord is my shepherd; I have what I need." (Psalm 23:1) As we look to our Lord and Savior, Jesus, we remember such comforting words as, "Come to me, all of you who are weary and carry heavy burdens, and I will give you rest" (Matthew 11:28). Or the hope giving words of the Apostle Paul in Philippians 4:6-7 when he writes, "Do not be anxious about anything, but in everything by prayer and supplication with thanksgiving let your requests be made known to God. And the peace of God, which surpasses all understanding, will guard your hearts and your minds in Christ Jesus."

If we are to relentlessly encourage others, it begins by us first going to God to be encouraged ourselves. The encouragement that comes from the Lord, His Word and His Gospel, give us the power, strength, and courage to look outwardly and enthusiastically to build up others who need it.

#2. We humbly accept God's exhortation to encourage others.

Hopefully by this point in the book, you are convinced there is no doubt God has called us to encourage! As we have seen, His Word is replete with commands to encourage. Let's be reminded of just a few passages:

"Therefore encourage one another with these words." - 1 Thessalonians 4:18

"Therefore encourage one another and build each other up as you are already doing."
- 1 Thessalonians 5:11

"Proclaim these things; encourage and rebuke with all authority. Let no one disregard you."
- Titus 2:15

"But encourage each other daily, while it is still called today, so that none of you is hardened by sin's deception." - Hebrews 3:13

God has clearly instructed us to encourage as we find encouragement in Him! What's wonderful and reassuring is that He always gives us His power to do what He has commanded us to do, to do what pleases Him (Philippians 2:13). We can count on it! Let's embrace God's admonition to encourage. Truthfully, what a gift it is to do so. Does He not encourage us daily through His Word and through prayer? As we are encouraged, we are to abundantly and consistently encourage others.

3. We trust the Holy Spirit to guide us, empower us, and give us encouraging words to speak.

Augustine once wrote, "Without the Spirit we can neither love God nor keep His commandments." He was absolutely right. Without the power of the Holy Spirit we are helpless when it comes to living a faithful, God-honoring, joy-filled, others-focused Christian life. We need far more of the Holy Spirit in our lives. Not less. We know from Scripture that the Holy Spirit:

- Convicts us of sin (John 16:8).
- Permanently indwells us (John 14:16-17).
- Seals us (Eph. 1:13).
- Teaches us (John 14:26).
- Guides us into all truth (John 16:13).
- Reminds us (John 14:26).
- Bears fruit through us (Gal. 5:22-23).
- Comforts us (John 16:7).
- Equips us with spiritual gifts (1 Cor. 12:4-7).

-    Empowers us (Acts 1:8).

The reality is that we absolutely cannot live as relentless encouragers in our own strength. It will happen only through the power the Holy Spirit gives us. We desperately need His power...

Power to guide us.

Power to overcome fear.

Power to lean into the awkward.

Power to follow through.

Power to speak the right words at the right time.

Corrie Ten Boom was right:

> Trying to do the Lord's work in your own strength is the most confusing, exhausting, and tedious of all work. But when you are filled with the Holy Spirit, then the ministry of Jesus just flows out of you.[15]

May we daily ask the Holy Spirit to fill us with His power, that Jesus' ministry of encouragement would flow out of us for the sake of others!

#4. We look for opportunities and then follow through in our encouragement.

As with anything God teaches us and commands us to do, the next step is to actually step out in faith and do it! We can talk about prayer, but ultimately God wants us to pray; He wants us to talk with Him. We can have a Bible, which is obviously good, but what God really wants is for us to open the Bible and actually read it. We can think about, write about, and even explain worship, but in the end, God has called us to actually worship Him. He wants us to sing His praises, offer our lives, give Him thanks!

This is true for encouragement too.

With God's help, we are to move from just reflecting on encouragement to actually encouraging someone. But we must work at it. It takes practice. With that in mind, let's look at different ways we can begin to daily practice relentless encouragement.

STRATEGIC WAYS TO PRACTICE RELENTLESS ENCOURAGEMENT

#1. Speak the truths of the gospel to others.

Those in our lives need to be reminded regularly of the good news of the Gospel. For the Christians in our lives, they need to be reminded over and over again of who they are in Christ and what He has done for them through His life, death, and resurrection. As relentless encouragers, we get to build others up by speaking these glorious truths that bring so much hope and encouragement. For our friends and family members who are not followers of Christ, they also need to hear the truths of the Gospel spoken to them with grace and love. Even if they seem to not be open to Jesus right now, God wants to use the message of the Gospel to save them and redeem them. We must not be ashamed or afraid because the Gospel alone "is the power of God that brings salvation to everyone who believes" (Rom. 1:16). Our only hope as sinners is found in Christ through the Gospel of grace! No message will ever be as encouraging as this one. We must be proclaimers of it to those around us.

#2. Privately build others up.

One of the most powerful ways to encourage others is by speaking to them genuinely and personally, one on one. If you have ever had someone pull you aside to speak an encouraging word to you, you know exactly what we are talking about. When we see an opportunity to encourage someone, let us take the time to pull them aside privately and build them up. God will use it!

#3. Publicly build others up.

While private encouragement is powerful, so is public encouragement. We need to practice both. As an example, my (Mark) daughter is getting ready to try out for a musical. She's been working so hard and has been practicing certain songs. Her voice is beautiful! I love listening to her. And she needs to hear me say to her, *"Babe, your voice is beautiful! The Lord has given you such a great voice."* You see, she's a bit insecure about her voice and is feeling unsure as to whether or not she should be in the musical. She needs to be encouraged, and my private encouragement to her, one on one, means a lot.

At the same time, at the dinner table, where we currently have family visiting us from out of town, I need to say for all to hear, *"Have you heard Zoe sing? She has a beautiful voice! I love listening to her! Her voice is such a blessing to our family!"* This is an example of moving from private to public encouragement. It allows others to join in the building up of a person!

Another example is with our staff at church. I need to be intentional to regularly say to our worship leader in private, "The way you led us in worship on Sunday was just incredible. The Lord totally used you." At the same time, I also want others to hear me say that about him so they can join in the encouragement: "Can we give it up for Ben today? Every week he leads us so well in worship. What a blessing you are to our church, Ben!"

Some people are better at giving encouragement in private than they are in public. Others are good at encouraging in public, but they're not very comfortable with encouraging in private. Relentless encouragers see the importance of both private and public encouragement and seek to grow in each of these for the building up of others.

#4. Remember the importance of cordiality.

What does it mean to be cordial? What is cordiality? The dictionary defines it as sincere affection and kindness. Being cordial with someone is to be kind in *how* we communicate. Sadly, cordiality, kindness, is so often missing in communication today. But, how important it is. In Colossians 4:6 (NLT) we read,

> Let your conversation be gracious and attractive so that you will have the right response for everyone.

Using manners, for example, is a very gracious, attractive, and cordial way to communicate with everyone. Be quick to say, "Thank you." Be kind and say, "Please." It stands out! When we are gracious and uncomplaining with a server at a restaurant, thankful toward the grocery store cashier, patient with those around us--when we are cordial with our words, our tone, and our body language, we reflect how patient, kind and gracious God is toward us.

#5. Quote Scripture to others.

Nothing is more encouraging than the truths and promises we find in the Word of God. In the midst of lies, pain, and insecurities that can seem to dominate us, we need to be regularly pointed back to the Scriptures and hear the voice of God speak truth and hope to us once again. Relentless encouragers are intentional to quote Scripture to those who need to be lifted up.

Relentless encouragers understand there is no better word than God's to build up the distressed and discouraged. While the Bible is filled with countless glorious, hope-filled, joy-producing truths to nurture our souls and the souls of others, here are a few passages to have ready to share:

> **Philippians 4:7** - "And the peace of God, which transcends all understanding, will guard your hearts and your minds in Christ Jesus."

> **Deuteronomy 31:6** - "Be strong and courageous. Do not be afraid or terrified because of them, for the LORD your God goes with you; he will never leave you nor forsake you."

1 Timothy 6:12 - "Fight the good fight of the faith. Take hold of the eternal life to which you were called when you made your good confession in the presence of many witnesses."

1 John 4:4 - "You, dear children, are from God and have overcome them, because the one who is in you is greater than the one who is in the world."

Psalm 28:6-7 - "Praise be to the LORD for He has heard my cry for mercy. The LORD is my strength and my shield; my heart trusts in him, and he helps me. My heart leaps for joy, and with my song I praise him."

Hebrews 12:1-3 - "Therefore, since we are surrounded by such a great cloud of witnesses, let us throw off everything that hinders and the sin that so easily entangles. And let us run with perseverance the race marked out for us, fixing our eyes on Jesus, the pioneer and perfecter of faith. For the joy set before him he endured the cross, scorning its shame, and sat down at the right hand of the throne of God. Consider him who endured such opposition from sinners, so that you will not grow weary and lose heart."

Psalm 46:1-3 - "God is our refuge and strength, an ever-present help in trouble. Therefore we will not fear, though the earth give way and the mountains fall into the heart of the sea, though its waters roar and foam and the mountains quake with their surging."

Isaiah 40:31 - "…but those who hope in the LORD will renew their strength. They will soar on wings like eagles; they will run and not grow weary, they will walk and not be faint."

1 Chronicles 16:11 - "Look to the LORD and his strength; seek his face always."

Hebrews 6:19 - "We have this hope as an anchor for the soul, firm and secure."

Romans 12:9-12 - "Love must be sincere. Hate what is evil; cling to what is good. Be devoted to one another in love. Honor one another above yourselves. Never be lacking in zeal, but keep your spiritual fervor, serving the Lord. Be joyful in hope, patient in affliction, faithful in prayer."

Hebrews 10:23 - "Let us hold unswervingly to the hope we profess, for he who promised is faithful."

1 Peter 5:7 - Cast all your anxieties on him because he cares for you.

#6. Avoid speaking as a superior.

No one likes to be spoken down to. No one. Not a child, not a spouse, not an employee, not a friend. No one. This is why we must avoid speaking as a superior.

Instead let us intentionally use "we" language. It's not "me" and "you"; it's "us."

For example, we have a pastor friend who could introduce himself on Sunday mornings with, *"Hi, I'm John, and I am the Senior Pastor here."* He could do that. It is true, afterall. But what does that communicate to the congregation? To other leaders in the church? To the other pastors and elders? It can be discouraging. It can subtly, even if unintentionally communicate, *"This is my church, and in case you didn't know, I'm the boss around here."*

Instead, a more humble and encouraging posture would be, *"Hi, I'm John and I am blessed to serve as one of the pastors of this great church. We have a team of great, godly leaders here and I am just blessed to serve alongside them."* What does this communicate? It says to everyone, "This isn't my church, this is the Lord's church and I'm simply blessed to be a part of it!" This is the posture and tone of a relentless encourager.

What might this look like in your life and leadership? In your areas of influence?

#7. Spend more time affirming and less time correcting.

What is your default? To affirm people or to correct them? To point out where others are succeeding or where they are falling short? It is important to take some time and honestly think about this. What does this say about what is going on in your heart?

Let's remember the wisdom we shared earlier from Chuck Swindoll who has said that as Christians, for every 1 correction we give somebody we should share 10 words of affirmation and encouragement. In other words, we should spend 10 times more energy affirming than we do correcting. Swindoll is exactly right. Of course, correction is important. At times, it is is very important. But let us make sure our correction of others actually makes an impact and leads to real change because it is rooted in the constant, ongoing encouragement we are first pouring into a person's life.

#8. Use a caring, loving tone.

This is huge when it comes to our words. Tone matters. Have you ever wondered why it is that a person can truly believe they are showing love to people and yet those very people do not feel loved by them at all? Or, perhaps a person speaks what they believe to be an encouraging word to someone and yet that person receives it as a criticism, not a word of encouragement? Or, why is it that some pastors, or leaders, or friends make you feel loved through their words, while others, who speak the very same words, make you want to cringe and run out of the room? Why is that? What is going on there?

It is often a matter of tone. You see, when it comes to encouragement, it is not simply a matter of the words you speak, it is a matter of the tone in which you speak them.

Do you ever think about your tone? It is something we each need to be aware of. In his book, *The Relationship Cure*, Dr. John Gottman reveals that when it comes to effective communication in our relationships with others, only 7% pertains to the actual words being spoken, while 38% comes from the tone of delivery. In other words, how others perceive and interpret what we are saying is often determined by the tone we are using. For this reason, we must regularly ask the Holy Spirit to make us sensitive to use helpful, loving tones when speaking to others. Here are some specific tones we must work to avoid in our communication:

- **Accusatory**: Charging of wrongdoing.

- **Apathetic**: Indifferent due to lack of energy or concern.

- **Bitter**: Exhibiting strong animosity as a result of pain or grief.

- **Bossy**: Controlling, selfish.

- **Cynical**: Questions the basic sincerity and goodness of people.

- **Condescending**: A feeling of superiority, patronizing.

- **Callous**: Unfeeling, insensitive to feelings of others.

- **Critical**: Quick to find fault.

- **Defensive**: Easily offended, not teachable.

- **Gloomy**: dark, discouraging.

- **Haughty**: Proud and vain to the point of arrogance.

- **Impatient**: Aggravated, self-focused.

- **Mocking**: Treating with contempt or ridicule.

- **Malicious**: Purposely hurtful, vengeful.

- **Pessimistic**: Seeing the worst side of things; no hope.

- **Ridiculing**: Putting down, making fun of.

- **Sarcastic**: Sneering, mocking.

Again, tone matters in our communication more than we realize. This is why we must be mindful of our tone if we hope to be effective in our encouragement of others.

#9. Be quick to apologize and ask for forgiveness.

How easy it is to justify our sin or to pass the blame of our sin onto others! Some of us live our entire lives this way, and we are miserable because of it. Both freedom and joy in the Lord come with taking responsibility for our sin. This is critical if we are to have a healthy, growing, vibrant relationship with God. As we read in 1 John 1:9, "*If we confess our sins, he is faithful and just and will forgive us our sins and purify us from all unrighteousness.*" Refusing to be honest about our sin before God will absolutely suck the life out of our relationship with Him.

This is just as true in our relationships with others—with our spouse, our kids, our friends, our bosses and co-workers, etc. How encouraging it is when you see someone who is quick to own their sin, apologize to others and ask for forgiveness. We must seek to demonstrate this kind of heart in our own lives. To own where we fall short and then quickly ask for forgiveness. It takes humility to say to someone, *"Please forgive me for _____."* Yet, this attitude is essential to living a life marked by love and encouragement.

#10. Pray for people when you are with them.

Have you ever been visiting with someone and had them offer to pray for you right then, right there, on the spot? I (Mark) have been blessed to be on the receiving end of these kinds of personal prayers on multiple occasions. To tell you the truth, it is difficult to think of times in my life when I have felt more loved and more encouraged than these. In fact, it happened just last week at our church. After our worship service, a kind, godly man in our congregation came up to me simply to encourage me and ask if he could pray for me. It was the highlight of my day!

As much as these prayers have meant to me over the years, I can imagine that others are just as encouraged when they are prayed for in this way. Talk about using your words to build others up! Instead of leaving a conversation with someone saying, *"I'll pray for you about that,"* pray for them right then, right there, on the spot. This is powerfully encouraging.

I was convicted a couple of years ago about this. I realized I had fallen into the habit of talking with people who would share a prayer concern with me, and I would say to them, "I'll be praying for you about that." The problem was, I would get distracted and fail to follow through on that promise to pray for them. I knew this had to change. In praying about it, I sensed the Lord leading me to change my message from, "I'll be praying for you" to "Let me pray for you right here, right now!" This simple shift was a game changer in my life and ministry to others.

It is one thing to tell people you will pray for them, it is entirely another when you pray for them on the spot. Whether on Sunday mornings at church, or at a weekly Bible Study, or when you are just hanging out with someone who needs prayer, let me encourage you to simply put your hand on their shoulder and say, "Can I pray for you right now? I know you're burdened by this, and I just want to go to the Lord on your behalf. Would that be OK?" This shouldn't be weird. It is what Christians do. We pray for one another. And let me tell you, it is one of the most loving and encouraging things we can do for each other.

#11. Be strategic with the five levels of encouragement.

As relentless encouragers, we should be looking for all kinds of different ways to build people up with our words. And the good news is that in our day, there are many different platforms we can utilize to share these words of encouragement. The question is, which platform is most effective? Let us propose what we simply call the "Five Levels of Encouragement." Each of these levels is represented by a different platform or pathway to be used when encouraging other people. In our experience, level one is often the least powerful form of encouragement, while level five is the most impactful. Let us briefly explain each level.

Level #1: Encouragement through Email. Encouraging people through email is great. There is nothing wrong with it. In fact, there are some people who prefer to be communicated with through email. The problem is that when it comes to encouragement, 1) email takes the least amount of effort, and 2) since many people check their email sporadically, they may not receive your encouragement in a timely manner. Again, email is ok, but we can do better. We may start at this level but let's not stay here!

Level #2: Encouragement through Text Message. More effective than email is encouraging others through text message. Why is this?
Text message allows for more personal and direct communication with someone and therefore more personal and powerful encouragement. Text messaging typically means that I have gotten to know a person on

a deep enough level that I now have their phone number. We are friends, or at least we are moving in that direction. Unlike email, when we text someone we can know that they will receive it quickly. It also allows for them to respond to the encouragement in a timely manner, perhaps allowing for an encouraging back and forth conversation through text.

Level #3: Encouragement through Handwritten Note. Handwritten notes are a lost commodity in our day. In fact, the giving and receiving of handwritten notes seems to be rarer and rarer. Whereas for centuries handwritten correspondence was a primary mode of communication, today it has largely been replaced by different forms of electronic communication. But this is not necessarily a good thing. As John Coleman writes,

> These electronic communications are rarely notable. But handwritten notes are unusual. They take minutes (or hours) to draft, each word carefully chosen with no "undo" or "autocorrect" to fall back on. Drafting one involves selecting stationery, paying for stamps, and visiting a mailbox. They indicate investment, and that very costliness indicates value. If, as the U.S. Postal Service notes, we only receive a handwritten letter once

every two months, each of those letters likely means more to us than the "cheaper" communication we receive each day.[16]

Handwritten notes are powerful. They stand out. They are personal. They take time and thought and intentionality. They are "above and beyond" in our day. Hands down, they are the most powerful form of written communication. This why handwritten notes are such an impactful way to encourage others.

Level #4: Encouragement through Phone Call. Still more powerful than email or text message or even handwritten note is encouraging someone through a phone call. The reason a phone call is so effective is because the other person can actually HEAR your voice as you encourage them. They can listen to your tone. They can hear the love and kindness and joy in your words toward them. As hard as one might try, an email or text message simply cannot capture this.

While fewer and fewer people regularly talk on the phone in our day, choosing to communicate through text message instead, relentless encouragers must fight this trend. We need to actually call people and encourage them! If it means we must leave a voice message, so be it. People need to HEAR encouragement spoken to them and a phone call is still the best way to make this happen. Unless of course you choose level five...

Level #5: Encouragement through Face-to-Face Interaction. Hands down the most powerful form of encouragement happens through face to face interaction. Face to face encouragement allows the person you are encouraging to not only hear your voice, but they can see your face as you build them up. More than that, your presence allows them to experience your sincerity and care in a way email, a text message, a handwritten note, and even a phone call simply cannot do. Plus, it allows you to give them a hug or a gentle pat on the back as an expression of your love for them. Nothing takes the place of face to face encouragement.

One last thing we want to point out. While all five of these platforms or pathways should be utilized in our encouragement of others, we should be mindful of which of these is most effective and meaningful for a particular individual at a particular time. This takes discernment. It might be that a person will feel most encouraged through a simple email or a text message. Perhaps a handwritten note or phone call is most appropriate. Whatever it might be, let us ask God to help us discern the most powerful and effective way we can encourage each individual.

#12. Receive encouragement graciously.

As strange as it may sound, one way we can encourage others is by graciously receiving their encouragement of us. Here's what we mean.

Have you ever been complimented or encouraged by someone and really didn't know how to respond? Of course you, have. We all have. Accepting words of affirmation and encouragement can feel uncomfortable, even awkward and perhaps a bit embarrassing. Because of this, most of us are not very good at receiving these words that are intended to build us up. The result is that often, whether we realize it or not, we end up robbing others of the joy of offering genuine encouragement to us. The loving thing to do is to humbly yet sincerely accept their words with thankfulness, encouraging them by receiving their encouragement of us.

So, how do we do this exactly?

Consider some great wisdom on this topic from Pastor Bob Kauflin. He shares four effective practices that have helped him in growing as a receiver of encouragement in his own life[17]:

First, thank the person just for taking the time to encourage you. Whether or not I think their compliment is sincere or warranted, they made a point of expressing their gratefulness. I don't have to know their motive or evaluate their grasp of reality. I can simply thank them.

Second, if someone's compliment is vague, ask them to be more specific. "Thanks for saying that! So what about the meeting encouraged you?" We're not fishing for more praise. It's just that God receives greater glory when we acknowledge how He worked specifically.

Third, express amazement and gratefulness for the way God works through any of us. "I'm so glad God encouraged you that way! Isn't He good?" What about the contributions of others? "Thanks so much. I'm just glad to be working with so many servants!" I often tell someone how much I've benefited from the example of people around me. One of the best ways to turn awkwardness into gratefulness is to remember how God has used others in my life.

Finally, and this is probably the most important thing, internally and intentionally "transfer the glory to God." That's a phrase I first learned from C.J. Mahaney, quoting the Puritan, Thomas Watson. It means telling God that whatever benefit, fruit, or glory is being ascribed to me at that moment is completely and rightfully His. I don't want it, because it's not mine.

We have found each of these insights to be incredibly helpful when receiving the heartfelt encouragement of others. Each of us must remember that God intends encouragement to be a gift of grace, both to those who give it and to those who receive it. Let us be mindful of this reality next time someone offers a word of encouragement to us.

BRINGING IT BACK FULL-CIRCLE

Let's remember the most important thing about the power and practice of encouragement: when it comes to the words we speak, the real issue is not our actual words but our hearts. It does not have as much to do with what our mouths say as it does with what our hearts love. As Jesus says in Luke 6:45, "The good person out of the good treasure of his heart produces good, and the evil person out of his evil treasure produces evil, for out of the abundance of the heart the mouth speaks." You can translate it, "Out of the OVERFLOW of the heart, the mouth speaks." What we say and how we say it is all about the heart.

The only way we are going to become individuals who speak words of true life and grace and encouragement is when we allow the Lord to take over our hearts. To transform our hearts. To change our desires, our affections, our passions, our very character, all by His grace alone. Only the Lord can do this in us, and He longs to do so!

DISCUSSION QUESTIONS

1. God is the Ultimate Encourager who gives us life-giving, life-changing truth through His Word. What are some passages that you have found to be particularly encouraging personally?

2. God clearly calls Christians to be encouragers. What does it look like practically to take Hebrews 3:13 seriously?

3. With God's strength and guidance, what are some specific ways you plan to practice relentless encouragement in your life?

CONCLUSION:

THE BARNABAS CHALLENGE

If you are not familiar with the disciple Barnabas in the New Testament, you need to be. Barnabas is one of those guys in Scripture that doesn't get a lot of air time but wherever he shows up we see an example of a relentless encourager! In fact, "Barnabas" wasn't his birth name (Joseph was his birth name), it was his nickname meaning "son of encouragement." In other words, Barnabas was so encouraging that it became his name. What a legacy to leave! Barnabas, "the son of encouragement."

To get to know this great encourager a little better, let's briefly look at a few key passages that give us a picture of who Barnabas was and how building others up was a primary mission and passion of his life. We are first introduced to Barnabas in Acts 4:32-37, where we read,

32 Now the full number of those who believed were of one heart and soul, and no one said that any of the things that belonged to him was his own, but they had everything in common. 33 And with great power the apostles were giving their testimony to the resurrection of the Lord Jesus, and great grace was upon them all. 34 There was not a needy person among them, for as many as were owners of lands or houses sold them and brought the proceeds of what was sold 35 and laid it at the apostles' feet, and it was distributed to each as any had need. 36 Thus Joseph, who was also called by the apostles Barnabas (which means son of encouragement), a Levite, a native of Cyprus, 37 sold a field that belonged to him and brought the money and laid it at the apostles' feet.

So here's the picture of what is happening in Acts 4. The early church in Jerusalem was growing like crazy. It was exploding with new converts. Lives were being transformed. All kinds of people were surrendering to Jesus as Savior and Lord. And to top it off, there was great unity in the church at this point. And because of that unity, there was great joy, and the Holy Spirit was working mightily in and through these early Christians. God was on the move! We also see that believers were selling their land and their possessions. They were then pooling their resources together so that everyone had enough food and that everyone's basic needs for life were being met. Notice that Verse 32 says, *"they had everything in common."*

In verse 36, we see Barnabas show up on the scene for the first time. He is part of this growing church and he is all in! As mentioned earlier, the Scripture tells us his real name was "Joseph." However, he was such a loving and generous and encouraging man that the Apostles changed his name to Barnabas, the "son of encouragement." Look at verse 37 of Acts 4 again. It tells us that Barnabas *"sold a field that belonged to him and brought the money and laid it at the apostles' feet."*

We see that Barnabas owned a good chunk of land, which is probably an indicator that he was a fairly wealthy man. Yet, out of his love for the Lord and for others, he sells his land and then gives all of the money he earned from it to the ministry, that the Gospel might spread. Right here is an example of how Barnabas was a humble man, a team player who loved Jesus and sought to encourage and build up those around him. How can you not love this guy!

But there is more that we learn about Barnabas. Our next encounter with him is in Acts 9:22-27, right after the Apostle Paul's conversion. We read,

> 22 But Saul increased all the more in strength, and confounded the Jews who lived in Damascus by proving that Jesus was the Christ. 23 When many days had passed, the Jews plotted to kill him, 24 but their plot became known to Saul. They were watching the gates day and night in order to kill him, 25 but his disciples took him by night and let him down through an opening in the wall, lowering him in a basket. 26 And when he had come to Jerusalem, he attempted to join the disciples. And they were all afraid of him, for they did not believe that he was a disciple. 27 But Barnabas took him and brought him to the apostles and declared to them how on the road he had seen the Lord, who spoke to him, and how at Damascus he had preached boldly in the name of Jesus.

This is an amazing scene! Saul (soon to be known as Paul) had been persecuting and killing Christians. Then, completely out of the blue, Jesus comes to Him on the road to Damascus and saves Him. He transforms His heart and makes him a new creation in Christ! And now, instead of wanting to kill followers of Jesus, he wants to join them in following Jesus.

But there was a problem. The believers in Jerusalem were well aware of how Saul had been killing Christians, which caused them to be very skeptical of his conversion. Was it genuine? Was his life truly changed? Could they really trust him? You can imagine the conversations, *"Listen, stay away from Saul. The guy is a liar. He is a fake. He's persecuting the church. And he will make sure we are persecuted as well."*

But then in the midst of all of this, Barnabas the encourager shows up. He comes alongside Saul, puts his arm around his shoulder, and says to the church, "Listen! This guy is for real! Jesus has changed Him! He's not our enemy, He is our brother. He is on our team. We need to treat him that way."

This is a picture of true encouragement. This is love. Barnabas was one of the first individuals to fully support and get behind the great Apostle Paul who the Lord would use in mighty ways for His glory. Such a reminder that everyone needs an encourager in their life. Even Paul!

A few chapters later Acts 11:19-24, we see Barnabas at work once again. We read,

162 THE RELENTLESS ENCOURAGER

> [19] Now those who were scattered because of the persecution that arose over Stephen traveled as far as Phoenicia and Cyprus and Antioch, speaking the word to no one except Jews. [20] But there were some of them, men of Cyprus and Cyrene, who on coming to Antioch spoke to the Hellenists also, preaching the Lord Jesus. [21] And the hand of the Lord was with them, and a great number who believed turned to the Lord. [22] The report of this came to the ears of the church in Jerusalem, and they sent Barnabas to Antioch. [23] When he came and saw the grace of God, he was glad, and he exhorted them all to remain faithful to the Lord with steadfast purpose, [24] for he was a good man, full of the Holy Spirit and of faith. And a great many people were added to the Lord.

We see here that Barnabas goes to this new church in Antioch with the sole purpose to love on and encourage the new believers there. He goes to encourage them in the Lord, to encourage them in their faith, to encourage them to stand strong even in the midst of trials and persecution that would surely come. He goes to shower them with words of Godly affirmation and encouragement.

What an example Barnabas is for each of us as believers. We could look at other examples of his encouragement in Scripture, but you get the picture.

God used Barnabas in huge ways to build up and strengthen others. Jesus has saved us and the Holy Spirit is conforming us into men and women who love and encourage others in the same way. We were made for it. And our world desperately needs it. Cindy Patten nails it when she writes,

> If you have a personal relationship with Christ, you have the same resources that Barnabas had. He had heard Jesus' message of salvation and glorious living through the power of God. Perhaps he was one who sat on the mountainside and heard the Great Teacher who spoke of His Father, of love, and of the promise of a blessed eternity. Perhaps he watched this same Jesus heal the blind and maimed and lavishly offer forgiveness of sins.

> Certainly he had spoken with the disciples and heard the marvelous accounts of their days with their great Friend. The reason Barnabas could be such an encourager to others is that he believed in the greatest Encourager! God is the "Father of mercies and the God of all encouragement". The grace of Jesus changed Barnabas into a son of the Father of encouragement! Like Father, like son. So, Barnabas learned to treat others the way God treated him. He knew the Source of encouragement, and he became a wonderful imitator of his Lord.

God's Word tells us that we, too, are to be imitators of Him in this same way.[18]

THE BARNABAS CHALLENGE: ENCOURAGE THREE

As we close this book, we want to offer you a challenge. While we hope and pray you have learned some new things and gained some new insights about the importance and power of encouragement, our ultimate desire is that what you have learned will translate into a life marked by intentional, relentless encouragement for the glory of God and the building up of others! For this reason, we want to invite you to take *The Barnabas Challenge.* Hopefully after learning a bit about this great encourager in the Bible, you can understand why we call it this. Just as Barnabas demonstrated a life of encouragement toward others, by God's grace, may we each seek to live the same way.

The Barnabas Challenge is very simple. You can summarize it in two words: **encourage three.** The Barnabas Challenge consists of purposely setting a goal of personally, specifically, and joyfully encouraging three people each day. That's it. That is the challenge. To make it part of the rhythm of your life, going out of your way to build others up by offering a word of encouragement to three different individuals each day. Of course, you may choose to encourage more than three, but make it a goal to encourage at least three people everyday.

You can do this! What you will find if you choose to take this challenge is a daily source of joy both for yourself and for those you encourage. This is what love does! Love brings joy. And as love spoken, encouragement is a pathway to genuine joy that only comes from the Lord. As Proverbs 16:24 says, "Pleasant words are a honeycomb, sweet to the soul and healing to the bones." May the words you speak, and the encouragement you give, be a source of sweetness and healing to everyone around you.

NOTES

[1] Charles Spurgeon, "The Rocky Fortress and Its Inhabitant," *spurgeongems.org*, accessed February 15, 2019, https://www.spurgeongems.org/vols28-30/chs1764.pdf.

[2] Tony Evans, *Tony Evans' Book of Illustrations: Stories, Quotes, and Anecdotes from More Than 30 Years of Preaching and Public Speaking, (Chicago, IL:* Moody Publishers, 2009), 77.

[3] Adapted from David Powlison, "Dealing with your Anger," *Family Life*, https://www.familylife.com/ articles/topics/life-issues/challenges/mental-and-emotional-issues/dealing-with-your-anger/

[4] J.A. Medders, "Jesus Cares About Your Words," February 23, 2016, https://jamedders.com/jesus-cares-about-your-words/, accessed May 15, 2019.

[5] Jon Bloom, "Enjoying a Good Laugh, Like God," Desiring God, https://www.desiringgod.org/articles/ enjoy-a-good-laugh-like-god, accessed March 7, 2019.

[6] Gerald Sittser, *Love One Another* (Downers Grove, IL: IVP, 2008), 22.

[7] Jon Bloom, "Breaking the Power of Shame," *Desiring God,* July 15, 2016, https://www.desiringgod.org/ articles/breaking-the-power-of-shame, accessed February 10, 2019.

[8] Russell Moore, "Is There a Loneliness Epidemic?" *Crosswalk,* https://www.crosswalk.com/blogs/ russellmoore/is-there-a-loneliness-epidemic.html, accessed February 10, 2019.

[9] John Piper, "We Need Each Other," *Desiring God,* April 19, 2017, https://www.desiringgod.org/messages/ we-need-each-other, accessed December 1, 2018.

[10] Rick Warren, "Be an Encourager at Work," *Oneplace.com,* December 17, 2018, https://www.oneplace.com/ministries/daily-hope/read/devotionals/daily-hope-with-rick-warren/be-an-encourager-at-work-daily-hope-with-rick-warren-december-17-2018-11802302.html, accessed June 6, 2019.

[11] Some of these suggestions have been adapted from C.J. Mahaney's excellent book, *Humility: True Greatness* (Colorado Springs, CO: Multnomah Publishers, 2005).

[12] Sammy Rhodes, "Don't Waste Your Awkwardness," *The Gospe. Coalition,* February 2, 2016, https://www.thegospelcoalition.org/article/excerpt-dont-waste-your-awkwardness/, accessed March 11, 2019.

[13] Tony Reinke, "Denzel: Your Phone is Changing You," *Desiring God,* May 19, 2017, https://www.desiringgod.org/articles/denzel-your-phone-is-changing-you, accessed March 10, 2019.

[14] Timothy Keller, *The Freedom of Self-Forgetfulness: The Path to True Christian Joy* (Chorley, England: 10Publishing, 2012), 31-32.

[15] Corrie Ten Boom, *Tramp for the Lord* (Fort Washington, PA: CLC Publishing, 1974), 63.

[16] John Coleman, "Handwritten Notes Are a Rare Commodity. They're Also More Important Than Ever." *HBR.org,* April 5, 2013, https://hbr.org/2013/04/ handwritten-notes-are-a-rare-c, accessed April 10, 2019.

[17] Bob Kauflin, "How do you receive encouragement?", *WorshipMatters.com,* March 3, 2006, https://worshipmatters.com/2006/03/03/how-do-you-receive-encouragement/, accessed March 10, 2019.

[18] Cindy Patten, "Becoming a Barnabas," Volume 21:3, *Journal of Biblical Counseling (JBC).*

foreword by Carl Trueman
author of Reformation: Yesterday, Today, and Tomorrow

SOLA

Mark Hallock & Ben Haley

SOLA

five 16th-century truths that
recaptured the heart of the gospel
and why they matter today

Mark Hallock & Ben Haley

FROM MARK HALLOCK

ACOMA PRESS

Acoma Press exists to make Jesus non-ignorable by equipping and encouraging churches through gospel-centered resources.

Toward this end, each purchase of an Acoma Press resource serves to catalyze disciple-making and to equip leaders in God's Church. In fact, a portion of your purchase goes directly to funding planting and replanting efforts in North America and beyond. To see more of our current resources, visit us at *acomapress.org*.

Thank you.

Made in the USA
Middletown, DE
27 October 2022